D1528010

*The Civilian Conservation Corps
in Arizona's Rim Country*

The Civilian Conservation Corps

in Arizona's Rim Country

Working in the Woods

Robert J. Moore

University of Nevada Press
Reno & Las Vegas

333. 75160979
M 82 c

University of Nevada Press, Reno, Nevada 89557 USA

Copyright © 2006 by University of Nevada Press

All rights reserved

Manufactured in the United States of America

Design by Louise OFarrell

Library of Congress Cataloging-in-Publication Data

Moore, Robert J. (Robert Joseph), 1949–
The Civilian Conservation Corps in Arizona's Rim Country :
working in the woods / Robert J. Moore.
p. cm.
Includes bibliographical references and index.
ISBN-13: 978-0-87417-677-3 (hardcover : alk. paper)
ISBN-10: 0-87417-677-8 (hardcover : alk. paper)
1. Civilian Conservation Corps (U.S.)—Arizona—Mogollon Rim—
History. 2. Civilian Conservation Corps (U.S.)—Arizona—White
Mountains—History. 3. Civilian Conservation Corps (U.S.)—
Arizona—Mogollon Rim—Officials and employees—Biography.
4. Civilian Conservation Corps (U.S.)—Arizona—White Mountains—
Officials and employees—Biography. I. Title.
S932.A6M66 2006
333.75'16097915—dc22   2006002132

First Printing

15   14   13   12   11   10   09   08   07   06   5   4   3   2   1

To Charles Pflugh, Marshall Wood, Eugene Gaddy,

Richard Thim, William Dean, Elmer E. Huber, and

the other young men who served in the Civilian

Conservation Corps in Arizona's Rim Country

Contents

For most of us, the Great Depression–era program called the Civilian Conservation Corps (CCC) rated a couple of paragraphs in our high school history book, and maybe a brief mention by the teacher about the number of trees planted in the forests by CCC workers. The college years didn't add much more information for me, even though my academic training focused on American history. It wasn't until much later that I came to realize the accomplishments, friendships, hardships, and good times that the young men of the CCC experienced.

During the summer of 1999 I was working as a seasonal interpretive ranger for the Apache-Sitgreaves National Forests in Arizona. Part of my job involved the development of historical displays at the Mogollon Rim Lakes Visitor Center, and I was searching for a topic for the next year's exhibit. Another Forest Service employee, Jim Mendell asked, "What about the CCC?" That simple question jump-started the project, which was aided by selected students from my American history class at Saguaro High School in Scottsdale, Arizona. The resulting display was set up at the visitor center in the summer of 2000.

The exhibit included the basic information about CCC work in the Mogollon Rim Country. I was very proud of the job my students did putting together selected photographs and an explanation of the simple elements of the program; there wasn't much room in the building for anything else. Long before the project was finished, however, it became clear to me that there was much more to tell.

That summer of '99, Jim Mendell also asked me if I wanted to see one of the CCC campsites. The buildings were long gone, of course, but the walkways and concrete foundations of Chevalon Canyon camp were still clearly visible. The pinyon-juniper country was open, clear, and little changed from the view the CCC boys would have had in 1939. Jim and I were the only ones at the site that afternoon. Standing in the middle of that empty camp in that silent forest, the questions came easily. Who were the young men who worked here? How did they feel about being so far away from home? What kind of work did they do? What was it like to live here? Where were they now? Had anyone ever told their story?

I wanted to find them. I wanted them to stand there with me at Chevalon Canyon and talk about their experiences. It must have been an adventure like no other. Yet, today the CCC is a benevolent but faded memory of American history. The individuals who participated in it are going fast, and their memories will one day be gone forever. I realized that their stories deserve attention before it is too late, but I barely knew where to begin looking for them.

As I delved into the history of the CCC in Arizona, I discovered that most of the enrollees were not local kids. After their CCC service, most had gone back East, participated in a world war, moved away from home, and settled down to raise their own families. Many were deceased. My search led me to the National Association of Civilian Conservation Corps Alumni (NACCCA), based in St. Louis, Missouri. This organization is the repository of manuscripts, photographs, and other memorabilia from CCC work around the country, but it has a policy against releasing names of members to the public. I explained my research motives, and after a series of convoluted and roundabout contacts, I one day received a telephone call from Charles Pflugh. He became the best friend I never met.

As a young man, Charlie had been a CCC enrollee at Chevalon Canyon camp—the same one I had visited that summer afternoon in 1999. He now lived with his family in West Virginia. Charlie was more than willing not only to share his experiences with me, but also to open up his family album and share photographs and unique souvenirs from his time out West during the Great Depression. I was taken aback by his generosity because I had been unsure how much information the veterans would want to share with a stranger.

Charlie's willing cooperation inspired me to try and find more of these men. I found a few, but it wasn't easy. I know I missed a few more, and I regret that very much. To my delight, however, I discovered that all the CCC vets I talked with were anxious to tell their stories and share their one-of-a-kind photos of camp life. The NACCCA has chapters all over the country where veterans, their wives, and interested citizens can meet and remember the CCC days. Chapter 44 is headquartered in Phoenix, Arizona. I found Richard Thim and Eugene Gaddy there. Both had worked at Blue camp in the White Mountains of eastern Arizona. Gaddy still lived next to the Blue River when I visited in 1999. I hadn't known him more than ninety minutes when he offered to put me up for the night. The CCC vets I met were that kind of people.

I placed a notice in the NACCCA's monthly newsletter asking anyone who had served in the forests of east-central Arizona to contact me. That is how I found Texas resident Marshall Wood. We talked on the phone, and he agreed to put his experiences down on paper for the first time. He sent his manuscript to me along with his photographs of CCC life on the Mogollon Rim. The CCC vets were that kind of people.

Although I searched every source possible, I found no other published material that told the story of the CCC boys who worked in Arizona's Rim Country. That knowledge made the stories I had unearthed even more precious to me, and also made me work harder to find other vets to interview. William Dean of Pennsylvania and Elmer Huber of California rewarded me with their experiences through letters and telephone conversations. Family members of deceased veterans who understood the significance of the contributions made by their loved ones came forward and shared their remembrances with me. I have included as much of their stories as I could piece together. The vast majority of the photographs in this book are from family albums rather than government archives. I shudder to think what might have happened to these treasures after the CCC men passed away. The photos might have been lost forever had surviving family members innocently overlooked their importance to history.

I am proud to present this collection of experiences from the CCC boys that might otherwise have been lost. The camp histories would have been pieced together eventually, but I consider myself fortunate to be able connect them to the veterans' stories in a way that presents a vivid snapshot of CCC life and work in Arizona's Rim Country during the Great Depression.

A final note. The Arizona Rim Country includes part of the White Mountain Apache Indian Reservation. CCC programs involving Native Americans were an afterthought among national organizing officials in 1933. The Native Americans who were enrolled were literally put into a class by themselves. The challenges involved in finding out about these enrollees are also in a class by themselves. For example, CCC project work for the Apaches was confined to the reservation; there were no permanent camps, and the few official records that exist are scattered.

Many, if not most, of the Apache enrollees of the 1930s were older than their non-native counterparts and are no longer alive. I found no manuscript collections of Native American CCC experiences on the White Mountain Apache Reservation. Tribal authorities and reservation officials familiar with local history knew of no White Mountain Apache CCC veteran that I could interview. If there are veterans out there, we need to find them and record their stories, perhaps in a separate study including common threads of experiences from other Arizona Indian reservations.

For now, I can tell only the story of the forest camps of the Mogollon Rim and White Mountains, and the men who lived and worked in these remote spots. Make no mistake; it is the human element that gives life and importance to the CCC. Some of the vets knew at the time that they were part of a grand and historical American experiment. I suspect that all of them know it now.

The first person I approached with the idea of putting together a special project on the CCC was Fred Green, Chief Recreation Ranger in 1999 for the Apache-Sitgreaves National Forests, Black Mesa Ranger District, in Overgaard, Arizona. Without that first boost of encouragement from Fred, the project might easily have fallen by the wayside.

Indeed, the Forest Service staff at Black Mesa District was more than accommodating. Besides Fred Green, I have Tim Grier, Heather Cooper Provencio, and District Ranger Kate Klein to thank for their support.

Arizona native Jim Mendell gave me my first tour of a CCC site. No one knows the forest of the Mogollon Plateau like Jim, and it was his input that gave me my first on-the-ground facts about CCC camps in the Rim Country.

Mel Schweigert from the Apache-Sitgreaves National Forests Supervisor's Office in Springerville analyzed historical photographs and provided archived names of CCC veterans. He was also my tour guide for later visits to several other CCC sites.

Clifton District Ranger Frank Hayes was helpful with information about the Eagle Creek and Juan Miller camps. Forest Service volunteer historian Kathleen Thomas was most generous in providing information that she had collected a few years earlier in her own research on the CCC companies that worked in eastern Arizona.

Archaeologist Michael Sullivan of the Tonto National Forest is an expert on CCC sites south of the Mogollon Rim and in the area around Payson, Arizona. His background information, access to historic photographs, and backcountry directions were invaluable.

John Irish from the Coconino National Forest shared one-of-a-kind file information he has collected over the years.

The best long-distance advice came from Gene Morris of the textual records division of the National Archives and Records Administration in College Park, Maryland. His patience with my odd questions, plus his research skills and knowledge, made him one of the most important people I talked with on this project. His efforts on my behalf saved many hours of tedious work. Nick Natanson of the Stills Processing Branch of the National Archives often went beyond my requests in order to increase my options for selecting the best photographs possible.

Most of all, there are the men of the CCC: Charles Pflugh, Eugene Gaddy, Richard Thim, Marshall Wood, E. E. Huber, William Dean, and the families of Fred Martin and Al Purdy. The veterans I spoke with were excited and cooperative. They held back nothing in their efforts to help me. Their stories of working in the woods are historic treasures, and I am honored to be their caretaker. Fred Martin's daughter, Kitty Butler of Payson, Arizona, opened her collection of old letters and photographs that added a personal touch to his service and made it possible to include his story. Ninety-two-year-old Elizabeth Purdy Fischer twice sorted through old newspaper clippings and family photographs to come up with details of her late husband's service in the CCC and Forest Service. Working with all of them to put together this book was the most rewarding part of the entire effort, and I will never forget them.

Many of those old veterans are also members of the National Association of Civilian Conservation Corps Alumni (NACCCA). Graduate student Julie Kemper at the main office in St. Louis was most cooperative in coming up with historic photographs and documents. Arizona Chapter 44 of the NACCCA provided me with important contacts to veterans and information as well. Others from that group provided encouragement and generously shared their ideas and knowledge of the CCC. Michael Smith serves as the volunteer coordinator for the organization. He is much too young to be a CCC vet, but he is the glue that holds the unit together. His dedication to the memory of the CCC is beyond anything else I saw during my research journey.

I turned to my brother-in-law Jim Krzeminski to help me get the old photographs from the various family albums onto the computer. Tech adviser Jeff Jordan and Saguaro High School (Scottsdale, Arizona) student Jason Thompson put in many volunteer hours organizing them on discs. I also called on my son Ty to solve last-minute computer problems.

At home, I disappeared every night to work on this project. Each night the hours flew by, and each night I realized that my work would not have been possible without the loving understanding of my wife, Lois. I hope she knows how grateful I am.

*The Civilian Conservation Corps
in Arizona's Rim Country*

Introduction

Relief from Hard Times

"It was the best years of my life." That is what many of the veterans of service in the Civilian Conservation Corps (CCC) say. It seems an ironic statement considering the fact that the CCC operated during the Great Depression of the 1930s, a time of grinding economic hardship that touched almost every family in America. Unemployment reached unprecedented levels, and so did the national sense of despair. Many household breadwinners became desperate for any job. Teenagers and young men wondered how they would ever get a start in life without a job or training in a special skill.

As the full weight of the Depression settled over the nation, popular demand for some type of relief program prompted newly elected President Franklin D. Roosevelt to act quickly. In 1933, during his first month in office, the Emergency Conservation Work Act was passed into law and the Civilian Conservation Corps was born. The CCC was a relief program whose purpose was to enlist unemployed young men between the ages of eighteen and twenty-five to work outdoors on forest and conservation-related projects. Enrollees had to be in good health and unmarried. They were paid thirty dollars a month, of which twenty-five had to be sent to relatives back home. The enlistment term was six months, but it was possible to reenlist for an additional term.[1]

Enrollment began in early April 1933, and by the end of that month— barely a month after Congress had approved Roosevelt's proposal—some camp locations had already been selected. The president appointed a civilian director to oversee the program, but the main responsibility for the day-to-day operation of the camps was in the hands of the U.S. Army. Everything was thus set up "the army way."

The prospect of military discipline and supervision by an army of-

1

ficer was not very appealing to many young men. In fact, most of the apprehension among potential enrollees and the later criticism of the CCC by outsiders centered on its military aspects rather than on its reason for existence. Drawn to the CCC for the job opportunities and adventure, however, the young men had no choice but to put up with the army's presence.[2]

Executive cabinet–level departments also had a hand in organizing the CCC. The U.S. Labor Department, for example, was charged with recruiting and processing the men. State agencies working with the Department of Labor developed a kind of quota system for supplying recruits. Most of the very early camps were set up in the eastern United States, close to a readily available workforce.[3] Afterward camps were set up in the West, where the vast majority of forestry jobs were located. Because fewer men lived in the Rocky Mountain states, however, it often happened that units of men were shipped from the East to jobs and camps farther west.

On enlisting, the men were given a general physical examination. They were then supposed to be sent to a military camp for conditioning and training, but that step was often bypassed. Next they were sent to a city or town that served as a regional staging area. Army officers would meet them at the depot and assign them to work units of about two hundred men. The men were usually grouped by town or region, and thus were able to serve with buddies and relatives from their home state no matter where the companies were sent.[4] After the companies were working in the forest, however, new enrollees were often assigned individually to fill slots opened by expired enlistments and desertions.

The CCC was a life-changing experience for the young men who gave it a chance. The corps provided an opportunity to mature into adulthood and learn interpersonal skills through hard work, friendship, and self-discipline. The administrators of the program knew the work and projects were important—that was the tangible benefit the government was seeking—and many government officials viewed the CCC as a success because of the work the men completed. But the visible brick-and-mortar work of the CCC is only part of the story. A significant part of the program's success is to be found in the life experiences of the young men who participated. It is their voices from the past that explain why these years were "the best of my life."

Thousands of the young men who enrolled in the CCC served in the forest camps in Arizona. Among them were Charlie Pflugh, Marshall

Wood, Eugene Gaddy, Richard Thim, William Dean, and E. E. Huber. Wood and Gaddy were both rugged Texas boys. Their Lone Star spirit and independence still shine through in their memories of work in the White Mountains of Arizona. As for Dean and Pflugh, everything west of the Mississippi River was new to them. They arrived in Arizona from civilized Pennsylvania, and both were experiencing their first taste of life out West. Richard Thim was a local kid from the farm country around Chandler, Arizona. He was used to farm work, but he thought it would be nice to be out on his own, earning money, helping his family, and getting out of the desert heat, all at the same time.

Although each man's story of life in the CCC is unique and special, all seemed to have a common set of goals when they signed up. Charlie Pflugh's goal was perhaps typical. Charlie was a skinny 113-pound youngster from the coal country west of Pittsburgh, Pennsylvania, when he joined the Civilian Conservation Corps in 1940. Nineteen-year-old Charlie was looking for excitement, and he thought the best way to find it would be to get away from home. Heading west seemed like an adventurous dream. "There was nothing wrong with my home life," he recalled, "but I was one of eleven children, and times were hard. I just saw this as a tremendous opportunity to see the country." He told the recruiting officer to "send me as far west as possible."[5] He got his wish. After a few days of processing and paperwork, he was on his way, assigned to join Company 3346 at Camp F-78-A—Chevalon Canyon—in the remote mountain plateau country of east-central Arizona.

Other government programs for youths have tried to duplicate the CCC's success. In the 1960s there was the Job Corps, and after that came the Youth Conservation Corps, which continues in modest form into the twenty-first century. Neither can compare with the CCC experience of the 1930s, however, perhaps largely because the later programs were not designed—or needed—to lift the crushing weight of economic disaster hanging over a nation of young men and their families.

Chapter 1

The CCC in Arizona

Much of the bureaucracy needed to get the CCC started already existed in the government. That convenience, combined with the program's altruistic objective, made the CCC initially less subject to legal scrutiny than some government programs. Other "alphabet agencies" designed to put the American economy back on its feet were also created in the first few months and years of the Roosevelt administration. Some were later declared void by the U.S. Supreme Court, and the usefulness of others was often criticized by a skeptical public. The CCC had its critics too, but most often their remarks dealt with its administration and control, not its mission.

The Department of the Interior was responsible for assigning specific CCC jobs to America's national parks and national monuments. In Arizona, officials at Grand Canyon National Park heartily embraced the idea of an army of workers that would put a shine on one of America's crown jewels. By the end of 1935, more than seven hundred young men were working in the park. Extensive trail maintenance and ambitious and very visible building projects, especially on the South Rim, drew new public attention to the range of activities and amenities one could enjoy at the canyon. Compared with similar work in the more remote national forest lands, park jobs were certainly more noticeable to the touring public. The goal at Grand Canyon was to use the CCC projects to attract more visitors, and that objective was met.[1]

The Forest Service branch of the U.S. Department of Agriculture directed more CCC work in Arizona than any other single government agency. As caretakers of the national forests (most of which are located in the West) it was the Forest Service, and not the army, that suggested specific projects to be completed on forest lands. CCC job assignments were recommended by regional and district rangers for each of the national forests, and rangers often trained and supervised enrollees working on these jobs. Especially in the early years, there were not enough foresters to provide all the supervision needed, so a call went out to forestry schools and colleges for supervisory personnel. The many people brought into the Forest Service in this way were an unintended benefit of the CCC program. Many rangers started their careers as CCC supervisors.[2]

At the organizational meetings held in Washington, D.C., when the program began, it was suggested that Arizona begin with an enrollment of one thousand men. That number was soon increased. Almost every company organized for duty in Arizona had reinforcement enrollees from New Mexico, Oklahoma, and Texas. Bringing "outsiders" into the state to fill out camp rosters was a practical manpower necessity, but the state's politicians took steps to look out for the local boys. Senator Henry Ashurst insisted that Arizonans recruited for the CCC be assigned only to camps and work projects in the Grand Canyon State. Ashurst wasn't able to keep all of the "undesirable" men from the East out of Arizona, however; in 1939, companies from as far away as Pennsylvania and New Jersey were sent to the state.[3] Thus, Charlie Pflugh and Bill Dean were among the few easterners to get a taste of Arizona living in the CCC camps.

Arizona had been a state for less than twenty-five years when the CCC program began. The state still depended on a rural economy and had an abundance of land administered by a variety of government agencies— a combination attractive to CCC directors looking for camp and work locations. It was both convenient and ultimately less controversial for officials to make use of public land (especially national forest land) for conservation projects. If the work was done on public land, there would be less likelihood that private landholders might benefit from government programs.[4] Some CCC work later spilled over and benefited private landowners, especially ranchers, but the abundance of federal land in Arizona was a major selling point at the beginning. Because the Forest Service was one of the first agencies to step forward with work requests, a large number of CCC camps appeared on national forest land.

There was no shortage of work to be done on the nation's forest lands. Typical CCC jobs in the western forests included trail and road building, construction of fire lookout towers and administration buildings, firefighting, soil and erosion control, and improvements to recreation

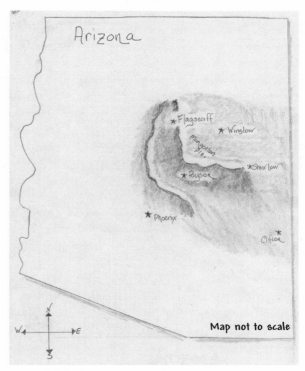

Arizona's Rim Country. Map by Ryan Deegan.

sites such as campground construction. The full impact of the CCC in Arizona went well beyond the national forests, however. The Bureau of Reclamation, the Fish and Wildlife Department, and even the War Department each had at least one camp in Arizona, and the Soil Conservation Service (SCS) camps were a major element of the bigger picture.

The SCS had more camps than any other government unit in Arizona except the Forest Service. Many of these camps were located in the lower-elevation ranch country of southeastern Arizona and the Gila River valley near Safford. Such camps were created partly in response to President Roosevelt's desire to alleviate Dust Bowl conditions, and partly as attempts to address the continuing problem of improper range management, soil fertility, and general erosion conditions on western grazing lands.[5]

The desert and lower-elevation SCS camps were a bonus for administrators of the Arizona program looking for an accommodating work cycle. Unlike many places around the country, work in Arizona was a year-round proposition: often the men worked at SCS camps in the desert during the winter and at forest camps in the Rim Country and White Mountains during the summer.

Year-round operations ensured an uninterrupted stream of cash and commerce flowing into the state over the life of the program. Although the enrollees sent most of their earnings home, government spending on the camp's transportation needs, supplies, and building materials was most often with local vendors, thus boosting the state's economy. The CCC boys built more than 5,700 miles of forest roads in Arizona, most of which are still in use. Besides roads, the CCC erected 3,559 miles of telephone lines throughout the state, an enormous benefit to the many Arizonans living in rural areas. More than 52,900 young men served in locations all over the state during the nine-year run of the CCC, and the program's contracts and work orders injected an estimated $60 million into the Arizona economy.[6]

The highlights the veterans recall of their service often involve the same things: making friends, taking trips, and hard work on the job. Many of the old-timers admit that those experiences were largely overshadowed by subsequent events. Most of the men went on to become part of the "greatest generation" that fought and won World War II.[7] Nevertheless, the CCC was for many their first away-from-home adventure, and their experiences in the camps made them more mature and prepared them for what they would have to face later, both on the battlefield and on the home front after the war. CCC enrollee Bill Dean said it for many recruits when he wrote,

> In 1942 when I enlisted into the 82nd Airborne Division and reported to basic training . . . my old CCC training really paid off. I was already familiar with barracks life and folded right in with the routine, unlike many of the new [non-CCC] recruits.[8]

Opportunities in the CCC were not as plentiful for ethnic minorities as they were for young white men. The law and its administrators professed racial equality and integration, but in practice, white and black enrollees were segregated in different camps whenever possible. Some camps were listed on the official record as "mixed" camps, but these were uncommon in the national CCC program. The few black men who served in mixed camps often were assigned as cooks or worked on cleanup crews or other less desirable camp jobs. A few of the forest

African American enrollees of Company 864. This detail from the full 1933 company picture at Bar X Ranch camp F-24-A shows that blacks were segregated for photographic purposes as well as other job assignments. Courtesy Eddie Blumer.

camps in Arizona included a small number of African Americans, but because few blacks lived in the West and the companies that came in later from out of state were already segregated, most camps in Arizona and elsewhere out West were white or a white-Hispanic mix.

Hit harder than others by the Depression, many Arizona Hispanics found both a home and hope in the CCC. Essentially all of the companies organized in Arizona at the start of the program included a significant percentage of Hispanic men—so much so that some camp newsletters were printed in Spanish as well as English. Although they shared the work routine, however, there is evidence suggesting that whites and Hispanics desired separate areas in which to socialize and relax.[9]

Among the truly overlooked minorities in the CCC were Native Americans. The White Mountain Apache Indian Reservation sits below the Mogollon Rim east of Young, Arizona, and in the western sections of the White Mountains. Today, the streams and lakes on the reservation are beautiful and pristine—a sportsman's paradise. The tribe takes care to guard against overuse and has a management plan for the land that limits camping, fishing, and other recreational opportunities in certain sensitive locations—all in the interest of conserving and preserving land and resources. That was not always the case.

Long before the Depression hit, the reservation was already something of a governmental backwater. The nature of the reservation system itself segregated Native Americans from the rest of society—so much so that historian William Collins noted that the Indians "generally lived in a world apart."[10] In the 1930s, drought conditions and exhausted cattle rangeland drove western reservations beyond the economic brink. The result was that unemployment and poverty rates were much higher for Native Americans than for the rest of the nation. Conservation was not a policy priority on Indian land. The Apaches and other Native Americans thus seemed to be good candidates for the kind of help Franklin Roosevelt offered in 1933.

Neglect and mismanagement at the local and federal levels may have contributed to the poor quality of life for the Native Americans, but administrators of the CCC did not ignore the problem. Nationally, more than fourteen thousand Native Americans signed on to serve in the Indian Division of the CCC. This separate category for Native Americans became a bit of a mixed blessing. Enrollment numbers were impressive on some reservations and adequate but uninspired on others. Yet the mere creation of an Indian Division suggested they were getting some attention. In the end, however, the Indian Division got lost in the bureaucratic shuffle.[11]

In terms of organization, the Bureau of Indian Affairs (BIA) of the Department of the Interior oversaw the CCC program for Native Americans. Management of the program on the Indian reservations was very different from standard CCC operations, mostly because of jurisdictional problems at the top government levels. The BIA jealously protected its authority over tribal work—to the extent that national CCC director Robert Fechner ended up having little control over the corps on the reservations. Rules and procedures were routinely bent. For example, the BIA and Office of Indian Affairs set and controlled their own enrollment numbers and procedures, and decreed that signups for Native Americans were to be open to all adult males regardless of age or marital status.[12] The men could also serve as long as they wanted. This policy was an obvious departure from the mainstream enlistment practices, but there was no apparent outcry of "foul" from political leaders or the general public.

Native Americans served in CCC companies with their own kind. For example, all crews working on the White Mountain Apache Reservation were members of the reservation's Apache tribe. The same was

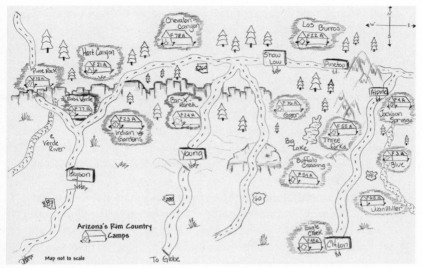

CCC camps in Arizona's Rim Country. Drawing by Ryan Deegan.

generally true of other tribes and reservations around the country. There was no racial mixing as was sometimes done with whites, Hispanics, and African Americans in forming mainstream companies. Job duties for the Apaches were almost always on the reservation, and the units did not mix with other CCC camps.

The Indian Division camp system had a different look as well. While work projects on the reservations were not greatly different from those of mainstream camps, it is hard to identify or document their accomplishments. Record keeping was what one national archivist called "a mess." On the White Mountain Apache Reservation there were no actual CCC camps. The enrollees simply lived at home on the reservation and went out every day to the job site.[13]

Veterans of those days on the Apache reservation are nearly impossible to find, for two reasons. First, because of the expanded age eligibility for Native Americans, many if not most of the Apache workers who signed on during the CCC days were beyond the age of thirty. Second, enrollment numbers on the White Mountain Apache Reservation were not particularly large. It therefore seems certain that the passage of so many years has taken most or all of them away from us.

All CCC camps throughout the nation were identified with a letter and number code. Camp codes usually had three parts: a letter, a number, and another letter; for example, camp F-78-A. The initial letter designated the type of camp (in this case forestry), the number was the camp number, and the last letter was the state location (i.e., Arizona).

Camp numbers were a record-keeping necessity, but the camps also took on individual names that were usually associated with their locale. Thus, in the forests of the Mogollon Rim there were camp names like East Verde, Chevalon Canyon,[14] and Indian Gardens. Even official reports used the local names. Camp sports teams, letter stationary, and the camp newspaper all used both the common name and the official designation. Conversations with old enrollees often begin with a mention of the common camp name rather than the official number as a way to jog the memory.

As for the camp buildings, the designs and layout bore the mark of the military. The army was responsible for camp construction, and shortly after the start of the program the army standardized the types of buildings the CCC would use. Yet it was not unusual or even objectionable that many Arizona camps did not hold strictly to the letter of construction plans. Factors such as slope, windbreaks, and unusual terrain were just as important as the standard army site plan in putting together a livable camp. Oftentimes actual construction was done by local laborers (not CCC enrollees), and even though the army supervised the work, site plans were altered for the sake of convenience.

An unidentified recruit at the entrance sign at Buffalo Crossing camp F-54-A, a favorite spot to stage a photograph for the folks back home. Courtesy National Association of Civilian Conservation Corps Alumni (NACCCA) Museum, St. Louis, Mo.

A person approaching a typical CCC camp might first notice the large wooden sign showing the camp's name and number. The sign became a favorite backdrop for photographs sent to the folks back home. The flagpole, nicely landscaped, was the camp's centerpiece. Behind the flagpole was the main administration building. Other necessary buildings were latrines, an infirmary, showers and wash area, kitchen and mess hall, officers' and enrollees' barracks, and garage and workshop. The standard CCC camp was designed to accommodate two hundred men.[15]

President Roosevelt wanted the CCC to promote the individual development of young men in addition to looking after the health of the national forests. Therefore, almost all of the main camps set aside or built a separate area for special educational or entertainment activities. The education adviser was one of the most important men in camp. His primary job was to organize classes and special activities for the men that were held mostly in the evening. L. W. Rogers, a past state superintendent of education for Texas, was in charge of the education program for CCC camps in Arizona and New Mexico. The program, he said, was

> not bound by any regular courses. One man is given what he needs or a group gets the course it wants. . . . We do try to place some emphasis on the vocational side, for many of these young men have no trades and come to the CCC camps because they had nowhere to go.[16]

Welding, auto repair, and heavy equipment operation were trades that could be put to good use when the enrollee went home as well as on the job for the CCC, and training classes in these areas were advertised that way to the boys. One camp newspaper reminded them:

> Before anyone decides whether to go home or reenlist, he should consider if there exists the possibility of his finding a job in his hometown. Many have received different kinds of training and should be in a better position to apply for a job when skilled labor is needed.[17]

Education advisers issued Certificates of Completion to those who successfully finished classes or training. These certificates could be used to identify skilled workers at camp, and former enrollees used them as reference documents when they were seeking employment back home after discharge from the CCC.

An enrollee had to be able to read and write before he could learn trade skills. Every camp with an education adviser offered courses in the "three R's." Many CCC old-timers remember men from their company (not themselves, of course) who attended those classes. The May 1940 issue of the Safford, Arizona, camp newspaper, *Noon Creek Echo,* reported that "fifty men raised their hands when Mr. Share, Education Advisor asked how many of those present had not gone farther than the third grade."

Paul Zengner, the education adviser at Pivot Rock (F-75-A) on the Coconino National Forest, went the extra mile to help his boys. He proudly reported in 1940 that all "illiterates" in camp attended classes four nights a week. Furthermore, he had worked out a deal with the Camp Verde School District (the company spent the winter in the Verde Valley) to award diplomas for CCC enrollees upon completion of eighth grade and high school graduation requirements.[18] Although they might have been embarrassed to admit it, hundreds, perhaps thousands, of young men learned to read and write in the CCC camps in Arizona.

The education building became a big part of Charlie Pflugh's life at Chevalon Canyon:

> We had an educational building that was used by the boys to sharpen their IQ. Being a high school graduate, I was asked to help those who needed it by teaching some of them reading and writing. There were a few boys in camp that came to me and asked me to write letters home for them. It was an embarrassment to them so I never told anyone else and will not mention their names now. Also, the education adviser, Manuel Puente, taught me the fundamentals of developing pictures and I became the camp photo processor. We even had a darkroom in the education building. (Pflugh letter, 2 October 1999)

Education was fine, but the boys were in the woods to work. In addition to trail and road building, erosion control, and other earth-moving work, many CCC jobs involved building structures. Fire lookout towers were perhaps the most important of these,[19] but construction of ranger stations and other Forest Service buildings was almost as significant.

Prior to the Depression, the Forest Service had begun standardizing the design of the buildings in its "administrative complexes" in the forest. Conformity, it was felt, enhanced the professionalism of the Forest Service by moving away from the haphazard design approach that had characterized ranger stations since the beginning of the twentieth

An enrollee from Indian Gardens camp F-23-A, east of Payson, uses his jackhammer skills to clear rock from FR 64, 1936. Courtesy Tonto National Forest.

century.[20] The standard plan for construction allowed a number of options, but the final design choice was made by the Forest Service regional office.

Region 3 (Arizona and New Mexico) planners liked the bungalow architectural style.[21] The bungalow style was a hugely popular house design during the 1920s, especially in California, and Forest Service buildings (ranger station offices, garages, etc.) constructed during the CCC days were largely of that type. Only a few remain. Structures built by the CCC for the district forest ranger can still be seen at Water Canyon on the Apache National Forest and at Pinedale on the Sitgreaves side.

The geography of the Apache and Sitgreaves national forests is dominated by the Mogollon Rim and volcano-uplifted White Mountains. The Rim has been called the second most spectacular geologic feature (behind the Grand Canyon, of course) in Arizona. From Sedona eastward to the New Mexico state line, the fossil-bearing sedimentary cliffs slice

View from the Mogollon Rim, 1939. Courtesy Coconino National Forest.

through half the state. From the Baker Butte fire lookout tower on top of the Rim, most of central Arizona opens up to the viewer—all the way to the San Francisco Mountains far to the north and the Colorado Plateau country of the Navajo Nation stretching away to the northeast. Looking south from the Rim it is possible to look past the Tonto Basin and Roosevelt Lake to the Pinal Mountains near Globe. East of the tower an ocean of green timber stretches to the horizon—the largest contiguous forest of ponderosa pine in America. This was the world in which Charlie Pflugh, Eugene Gaddy, Richard Thim, Marshall Wood, Fred Martin, and other young CCC enrollees found themselves.

"My love affair with Arizona began in September 1934, when I first came to the state because of the Civilian Conservation Corps," wrote Elizabeth (Betty) Purdy, whose husband, Al, was an enrollee who stayed on with the Forest Service after his enlistment expired. Of her first ride into the mountains she said:

> That trip was thrilling enough, but when we got to the Alpine area it was even better . . . believe me, I had never seen such beautiful country as the White Mountain region.[22]

Summer work conditions on the Mogollon Rim and White Mountains are almost ideal. May and June, typically dry months, allow uninterrupted work with comfortable daytime temperatures. July and August are usually two of Arizona's wettest months. Monsoon flow from the south generates towering cloud buildups by late morning with strong thunderstorms breaking over the mountains and Rim by late afternoon and into the evening. The pattern repeats almost daily. The storms are often violent and the rainfall heavy, but they generally don't last long. In most cases the rain interrupted only part of a day's work for CCC crews. The dry air returns in September and October, and even though it is autumn in the woods, daytime temperatures are still pleasant. Winters have their share of unpredictable weather, and the nights can be bitterly cold. Blue and Chevalon were the only CCC camps in east-central Arizona that were built and equipped for cold-weather occupation. Eugene Gaddy and Richard Thim experienced winter duty at Blue CCC camp, while Charlie Pflugh endured a winter season at Chevalon Canyon.

Summer or winter, the U.S. Forest Service saw the CCC as a useful tool for opening up the forests of central and eastern Arizona to increased recreation use.[23] Many Phoenix residents had already established a favorite recreation route to escape the desert heat. Prescott had been a preferred summer destination since the early pioneer days, and the route north from heat-oppressed Phoenix and the Valley of the Sun was well known and well traveled. For the motoring public of the 1930s looking for a weekend camping getaway, the Mogollon Rim–White Mountains area was a remote and little-visited destination.

Before the CCC went to work, most of the visitors to the White Mountains and eastern Mogollon Rim came from the small Mormon communities in the region and the railroad towns of Holbrook and Winslow.

Al Purdy at Blue camp F-03-A, 1934. Mail was the enrollees' lifeline to the outside world. Courtesy Elizabeth Purdy Fischer

From the Holbrook and Winslow side, getting to the cool pines required a forty-five-mile trip on a dirt road across the treeless high desert of the Colorado Plateau. Copper miners from Clifton looking for a camping adventure sometimes tried the narrow, winding climb uphill to the southern sections of the Apache Forest, but it was an arduous undertaking. Nobody expected campsites with tables, water, or toilet facilities. By the end of the CCC era, a wilderness experience was still possible, but crews of young men had created a number of developed campsites with family-friendly conveniences and auto access.

Some CCC work not originally intended as a recreation project later had a big impact on forest visitation. Road construction during the CCC days was almost always related to fire suppression, with the goal of quickly getting men to the source of the smoke. Afterward, these fire roads turned into numbered forest roads that opened up the backcountry to recreation uses. A good example is Forest Road (FR) 64 (Control Road) on the Tonto National Forest below the Rim running between Kohl's Ranch and the towns of Pine and Strawberry. It started as a fire road and continues to serve that purpose. Indeed, this road was the primary access for firefighters fighting the devastating Dude fire of 1990. But CCC improvements to FR 64 had the longer-term effect of opening the area to recreational use on a grand scale. The Control Road, once a tortuous route to pioneer homesteads, is now an easy drive leading to summer homes, a Boy Scout camp, hiking trails to the top of the Rim, and a section of the woods that has become a favorite spot for rock hounds searching for "Arizona diamonds" (clear quartz crystals).

CCC improvements on existing roads in the forest also helped pull visitors into the woods. This was most true of the Old Rim Road stretching east and west across the Mogollon Rim in the Coconino and Sitgreaves national forests. Pioneered as the General Crook Trail in 1871, it was nothing more than a narrow wagon road during the Indian War days of the 1880s and the early years of the twentieth century. The Forest Service went to work on it in 1909, and in 1928 it received another overhaul. CCC crews further improved it in 1933 as part of a fire control road system. Eventually the road became a recreation access point that boomed with visitor traffic after State Highway 260 was paved from Payson to the top of the Rim and several lakes were built in the 1950s and 1960s. The width and condition of FR 300 have changed little since the CCC improvements. It remains a slow yet pleasant cross-forest auto trip that features some of the best mountain vistas in the state.

Fire was serious business for forest managers. To the Forest Service, successful firefighting in the mountains required trained firefighters and roads to get them to the fires. Both parts of the equation were necessary. For example, in 1937, seven fires in the area north of Clifton burned several hundred acres merely because there were no adequate roads to get crews in to fight the flames.[24] The Forest Service was overjoyed to have a corps of men readily available and reasonably close to whatever wildfires might erupt, and rangers did not hesitate to make generous use of CCC crews for firefighting purposes. Almost all camps offered some type of fire training classes, but each developed its own fire training regimen; the degree of proficiency often depended on the experience of the Forest Service official offering the training.

Bill Dean signed up for the CCC in 1940, a week after graduating from Steelton High School in central Pennsylvania near Harrisburg. Finding a job was a motivating factor. "The coal mines and steel mills were awful quiet," he recalled. He was soon on a train heading for adventure in one of the newest Arizona camps, F-80-A located a few miles northwest of Flagstaff. Bill especially remembers his service fighting fires. He didn't get much training, but every time he went out he picked up more experience. He knew how to handle the basics of wildland firefighting, and he knew help was nearby if he needed it:

> Whenever a forest fire got going in the Coconino National Forest, we were loaded in trucks and became firefighters. Alongside us were the Zuni Indian tribal firemen. They always jumped in to help us. I think in some cases they were already at the fire by the time we got there. Our job was to cut fire breaks in the light brush, and if the wind was right we would start a backfire. (Dean letter, 20 April 2001)

Fighting the fire was not always Dean's primary concern. While working on the fire line one time, he heard a strange noise apart from the fire but coming from the same direction as the smoke. Apparently Bill had not received instruction about the behavior of wild animals caught in a forest blaze.

> Burned into my memory is the overwhelming fear I felt seeing wild-eyed, panic-stricken bear, deer, fox, etc. running out of the fire (some with smoke coming off their fur). They were coming right at me. Somehow that twelve-inch-diameter tree I jumped behind seemed like a broomstick. (Dean letter, 20 April 2001)

Regardless of where they worked on the forest, almost all of the CCC boys got a chance to put their firefighting training to use before their enlistments were up. Charlie Pflugh recalled the importance of fire duty at Chevalon Canyon:

> When I was out working with Francis Bealey we were part of the Timber Stand Improvement unit. That included trimming trees, planting of seedlings, and fire control when needed. The urgency of the job pretty much dictated what job you might do each week. Of course a forest fire involved all men that could be spared from other duties. While there were only a few fires while I was there, the mere threat of a fire was a major concern to the Forest Service. They would not hesitate to take men off other jobs to work on fires. I was at a side camp near Clay Springs one time. That was quite a ways from the main camp. We spent a lot of our time clearing dead wood and making a right-of-way, but part of the reason we were there was for fire control. If something popped up, we would be close enough to deal with it. (Pflugh interview, 4 November 1999)

Managing a CCC camp of two hundred young men was no small task. It required an experienced organizer. That is why overall command of a camp was placed in the hands of a military officer (usually a lieutenant or captain), often one from the reserve ranks. There was also a military second in command, and most of the main camps had a military doctor as well. The army was generally responsible for the men from 5:00 PM until 6:00 AM. A normal workday for the enrollees began at 6:00 AM, with roll call at 6:20 and breakfast at 6:30. Work call was at 7:30, lunch was at noon, and dinner was at 5:30 PM. The men then had time to themselves until lights out at 10:00 PM.[25] Charlie Pflugh remembers his camp as being very military:

> I personally thought Chevalon Canyon camp had an outstanding group of officers and foremen. . . . Since the army was in charge, you played by their rules or else you suffered for it by doing extra KP, latrine duty, cleaning out the garbage pit, losing your weekend pass, and being confined to barracks. (Pflugh letter, 4 November 1999)

Understandably, the men sought ways to break up the routine, especially during the idle hours around camp. That was not easy in a camp

Lt. Elmer E. Huber, the army officer assigned as second in command at Blue camp F-03-A, 1936. Courtesy E. E. Huber.

in the middle of nowhere. But the men usually found a way. Those who wanted to sample something different, or at least something other than the military-issue basics, went to the camp canteen, a kind of general store that sold candy bars, razor blades, and other items not a part of the usual CCC rations or government issues. Most camps had them, and they became a popular stop for enrollees looking for that something special to buy.

The way the canteen worked at the Bar X Ranch camp was typical. Business partners Elvis Clark and Alphie Rascoe ran the general store in Young, Arizona, eight miles south of the camp. When they heard that a CCC camp was to be located nearby, they contacted federal authorities. The government awarded them a contract to set up a tent "outlet" at the camp to supply enrollees with basic personal items beyond the usual army issue. Some of the canteens were nicely framed buildings consistent with other structures at the camp. The one at Bar X was simply a walled tent, but that didn't matter to the men.

Like a rural post office or community store, the camp canteen became a gathering point and social center. No alcohol was served, but those with a little extra money in their pockets could find a special treat or snack. In the few short months that the Bar X Ranch camp existed, Clark and Rascoe got to know the enrollees quite well. The two businessmen profited in another way, too. Camp commanders contracted locally for perishable foods for camp meals, and the canteen proprietors made additional money by meeting that need.[26]

Charlie Pflugh has fond memories of the Chevalon Canyon canteen, a place where one could find small pleasures:

Another building that was used a lot was the canteen. Candy and pop were the big items. In those days the good candy bars were five cents. That was also true of the soda pop. To me, the portions were much larger than the candy bars of today. We really looked forward to going there. Many of my friends said that the trip to the canteen was like candy from home. (Pflugh interview, 4 November 1999)

Work projects depended on experienced foremen to guide and train the young men when they left camp to go out in the woods and begin work. These "local experienced men," or LEMs, served as technical supervisors, foremen, and skilled instructors, and the CCC would not have been nearly as successful without them. The LEMs had separate work contracts and were not classed as enrollees. Their jobs, created through a directive from national CCC headquarters, were partly intended to placate local communities who viewed CCC workers as outsiders taking jobs away from townspeople who needed them just as much.[27] Depending on their skills, these local men were sometimes moved from camp to camp rather than being permanently attached to a particular CCC company.[28]

The LEMs had a wealth of trade skills that could be passed on to the enrollees. Their greatest value to the CCC was as instructors for the young men who had little experience in outdoor life or heavy equipment operation. The 30 March 1936 edition of the *Eagle's Nest,* the camp newspaper for Eagle Creek on the Apache Forest, said exactly that:

> Probably the biggest benefit . . . has been the instruction given the men on the job by the foreman. During the Depression, it has been impossible for us to find an opportunity in commercial life to get any actual training as an apprentice in the various trade positions.

These newfound skills would help the men get jobs after their CCC service ended.

An ambitious enrollee who followed the right advice found it easy to climb the learning ladder with help from LEMs and Forest Service supervisors. Recent high school graduate Bill Dean was "green as grass" when he reported for duty at Flagstaff:

> I never drove before, but after a month in camp I was driving a dump truck. A short time later I became a "grease monkey" run-

ning the trucks up on a homemade log ramp and using a "by hand" grease gun to lubricate the vehicles. A few weeks after that I was in forest ranger Frank Randall's "experimental forest" as a chain man with a surveying crew. (Dean letter, 20 April 2001)

Perhaps typical of the LEM experience was Fred Martin's work for the CCC. A native Arizonan, Fred grew up in the Round Valley community of Springerville, the gateway town to the White Mountains. His father, a Forest Service supervisor, owned a beautiful ranch near Eager. In the late 1920s, telephone crews came through town, connecting the area to the rest of the world. They were also looking for men to help with the work. That was Fred's chance to develop a skill, so off he went with the phone company. Some of his duties took him out of state, but by the time the first CCC camps were built in 1933 Fred was back in Round Val-

Grease rack at Indian Gardens camp F-23-A, July 1934. This maintenance lift was typical of those found at many camps in the Rim Country. Courtesy Tonto National Forest.

ley, still with the phone company. His skill as a lineman and his knowledge of the woods got him hired as a LEM in the Civilian Conservation Corps. Fred was sent out to work at the Blue River camp, southeast of Alpine in the heart of the White Mountains.

Fred's specialty was telephone line construction, and he stayed with the CCC for nearly the full nine-year run of the program (in contrast to the standard six-month term for traditional enrollees). From the Blue camp he followed the workers to their CCC summer camp at Buffalo Crossing. There was plenty of work to be done. The Forest Service wanted phone lines run to each of their ranger stations and connections to the Blue, Green's Peak, and Reno fire towers.

There were occasions when Fred was needed in more than one place at a time. In 1939 his fence-building crew near Big Lake was left to complete that work while Fred was called away to supervise road construction on Forest Road 276, a main route into Buffalo Crossing.

Fred's CCC days also included a long-distance correspondence with his wife-to-be, Kitty Gaither. Their romance flourished, and Fred and Kitty were married in 1939. The CCC's need for his services did not end with his marriage. The Martins were assigned living quarters at the camp—something that would have been forbidden to a common enrollee. A small site on the outskirts of camp became a family neighborhood. Fred Martin's son Charles was born and spent his early childhood at Buffalo Crossing camp in the White Mountains. Fred's parents visited from Texas and picnicked in the woods nearby. Those reminders of family life must have tugged at the heartstrings of the homesick enrollees.

Fred's telephone construction crews became a sought-after assignment for the young men of the camp. That was partly because telephone work seemed like easy duty compared with the rigors of roadwork, which involved boulder removal and heavy equipment operation as part of road construction and stream improvement projects. Fred's day didn't end when the trucks came back to camp, either. By 1935 he was also in the CCC classroom teaching a well-attended class on telephone line construction as part of the educational program at Blue camp—just another part of a day's work for a LEM.[29]

With the possible exception of Los Burros camp, located two miles from Pinetop (population four hundred in 1936), all of the CCC camps in the White Mountains and Mogollon Rim Country were far removed from town conveniences. Camp commanders were well aware of what the isolation could do to the boys. Certainly there were opportunities for

Fred Martin, local experienced man (LEM), mid-1930s. Courtesy Kitty Butler.

enrollees to get away for a weekend, but many of them, far from home for the first time, had nowhere to go. Most of the companies serving in the White Mountains and Rim Country had few native Arizona boys—and even they were oftentimes unfamiliar with the mountain country.

At first, the sheer adventure of being on their own in the wilderness kept the fellows going, but the isolation slowly closed in. Canyons and miles of tall ponderosa pines surrounded the boys. Sure, they had joined up with a couple of buddies from back home, but there were two hundred other men in camp—a lot of strangers to deal with. Even if everybody got along, these friendships weren't always enough to overcome the loneliness. No part of Arizona's forest country looked like back home for the Texans. Isolation, strange surroundings, and homesickness prompted a few of the young men to "go over the hill" and head for home. Special Investigator M. J. Bowen, who was responsible for official inspections at several camps on the Mogollon Rim and White Mountains, reported in 1940: "I am sure that the Texas enrollees have all other states beaten on desertions, at least all the states I travel."

Marshall Wood was an enrollee from Texas who served at Los Burros—one of the first CCC camps set up in Arizona. He recalled the isolation:

Things were so bad those first few weeks that many of the guys couldn't take it. They just left and didn't come back. We lost a lot of guys that way. Anyway, after a month or so, we got replacements who were Arizona boys.[30]

Desertion problems at Pivot Rock camp (F-75-A) on the Coconino National Forest southeast of Flagstaff were chronic. Official reports called the camp "tremendously isolated." Commanders were amazed that deserting Texas boys who left camp on foot somehow managed to make their way out of the woods and back home on their own. The district commander, Lt. Col. R. Gordon, was informed of the problem during an inspection tour of Pivot Rock in June 1941 and promised to "try and send each enrollee to Flagstaff at least once a month" as a way to relieve the isolation at the camp.[31]

The CCC camp at Buffalo Crossing was in a beautiful setting, a "splendid location for a camp site." As an official report noted, however, being in the middle of the White Mountains made recreation opportunities for the young men "somewhat of a problem." Nearby towns were small, and trucks were not always available to take the men in on weekends. Desertions by homesick boys from Texas were "very high." One young man who decided to go over the hill from Buffalo Crossing was on the road hiking into town when he happened to meet the camp's army commander driving back to the work center on the same road. One can imagine the conversation that took place. The official record simple states that the boss got him to return after "talking to him for some time."[32]

The men were able to get leave time to go home and visit their folks, and most camp commanders were generous with passes. But distance was a factor in how often a fellow could get away and how far he could go. CCC administrators tried not to ship young men across the country for duty because it created problems getting home. Some suspected that giving furloughs to enrollees who lived great distances from camp would tempt them to stay home and never return to service. Keeping track of local boys was an easier proposition. It was generally understood that enrollees whose hometown was nearby could get leave once a month. Reenlistment enrollees got six days' leave between tours. It was all designed to help alleviate the disease called homesickness. Regardless of how much they suffered, though, the boys who stuck it out generally agreed that their experience in the camps had been a character builder.

Chapter 2

A History of the CCC Camps
in Arizona's Rim Country

At the start of the CCC program in 1933, the army made plans to open twenty-eight camps in Arizona. The forest rangers assigned to supervise the work projects were given great latitude in choosing precise camp locations. Proximity to work projects plus the means to get supplies to the men were major considerations, but not the most important one. Availability of water was the number one factor determining exactly where a CCC camp would be set up. The army had the power to accept or veto exact site locations, and the chief reason for rejection was lack of water. Hardworking young men can do without many things for a time, but not water. A fully manned camp could use three thousand gallons of water a day—and even more in the desert. One desert site in the Gila River valley was closed after one year because of water problems, despite the fact that permanent masonry barracks had been constructed.[1]

There is no record indicating that any camp locations in the White Mountains or Rim Country were rejected. Indeed, the plentiful water was probably one reason why so many CCC camps were placed there. The mountain camps of the Rim Country and eastern Arizona could tap into a number of streams and mountain springs, and there was well water available as a backup. Official inspection reports from Indian Gardens, east of Payson, said the camp's water supply from a spring was "abundant." It is easy to imagine the boys taking a break at Buffalo Crossing on the Black River, or young men working along the East Verde River dipping their cups into a cold, refreshing stream and enjoying the pleasures of working outdoors in the high country.

Although mountain water was reputed to be clear and pure, the army and Forest Service took no chances. All water used in the camps was chemically treated. There were complaints aplenty about the chlorinated taste, but camp officials and national administrators stuck to the policy.

Fourteen main camps were established in the White Mountains and along the Mogollon Rim by the CCC (see appendix 1). While only a few of them were occupied year-round, for official records purposes they were given the number identification and status of main camps.

BLUE (F-03-A)

The camp was located at the mouth of Johnson Canyon along the Blue River, deep in the mountains of eastern Arizona. A more remote site could hardly have been found. Mountain wilderness extended for miles in every direction. For all practical purposes, there was one way in and out of Blue camp. The site was intended as winter quarters despite the forested location, so the facility was constructed from the beginning as wood-frame barracks instead of tents. The camp thus had a sense of permanence that must have looked odd to the few ranchers in the valley who knew how far away they truly were from civilization.

The original staging area and closest railhead for Blue was at Silver City, New Mexico, more than 130 miles away. Supplies came in over rough and unpaved forest roads from that location. After the camp had been open for two years, two army trucks were on the road almost daily bringing in rations and supplies. Most CCC camps in the region were allowed fifteen hundred dollars per week for grocery staples, but the Blue camp was given twenty-five hundred to ensure a supply of staple foods as a hedge against the distance and difficulty of getting goods to the camp. Anyone at camp in need of serious medical attention was driven back over those same rough roads to the hospital at Fort Bayard, New Mexico.

A newspaper reporter in 1934 wrote that "Blue, Ariz. is the most isolated camp in these United States." Even as late as 1941, when road construction had shortened the distance to the other towns, a CCC investigator looking into a "group discharge" for several men found that the isolation of the camp was the true reason for their refusal to work and their subsequent discharge request.[2]

Despite its remote location in the heart of the Apache National Forest, the Blue camp was one of the most active and most important of

Blue camp F-03-A, 1941. Courtesy Richard Thim.

the CCC camps in eastern Arizona. The first company reported there in June 1933, making it also one of the first camps. The unit worked in the area until 1941, shifting back and forth between Blue and the summer camp at Buffalo Crossing. Thus, the camp was in operation for the entire length of the national CCC program. This was very unusual in the forests of the western United States, where camps were routinely closed and companies reassigned to other camps closer to new work areas. The long-term occupation of the Blue camp is an indication of the amount of work that needed to be done in the area, and the men who served there get credit for a large volume of completed projects—so many, in fact, that it is not possible to identify them all. But a few are still visible on the forest.

In the early days of the camp, construction of telephone lines and roads to the outside world was a top priority. One of the first projects was construction of Forest Road (FR) 232 from Blue eastward. A CCC unit from Pueblo Park was working west from their camp in New Mexico. Blue camp's Company 842 faced an uphill twelve-mile forested mountainside. It's no wonder that there was ceremony, celebration, and handshakes all around when the two road crews finally met.

Among the most notable work projects coming from F-03-A were the bridges constructed over the Blue River upriver and downriver from the camp. At one time, crews were working on three bridges at once. The unbridged sections of FR 281 from the camp north to State Highway 180 also had to be maintained after occasional washouts. This was important because this route was the closest access to the towns of Alpine and Springerville.

Another major road construction project was the narrow Red Hill Road (FR 567) leading from the Blue River northwest to State Highway 191. Uphill from the camp, it became something of a bad luck assignment. The camp newspaper reported equipment problems and worker injuries (mostly minor) during construction on this road but mentioned very little about mishaps on other projects.[3] An incident that occurred during construction of FR 567 is a good example of the showoff bravado some of the young men exhibited in their work.

Enrollee Marion Watson, a dump truck driver, had a difficult time turning his truck around after dropping off its load of gravel. "You couldn't make any mistakes on that road because there were places with a thousand-foot drop-off down the bank," he later said. Watson played it safe by continuing on to a wider section of the road before turning around. When he realized that the other drivers were turning around at the dangerous narrow spot where they had dropped their load, though, he decided "if they could do it, so could he—and he did."[4]

Camp officials did not ignore such reckless behavior on the job. Blue camp had a safety committee that met twice a month. The camp's safety record was a bit lax when compared with other units on the Rim, but they were trying to improve. Al Purdy was the lead instructor for the road construction class, and official reports noted that the class "has been the most gratifying during the month. Nearly all the members are leaders."[5]

Along the Blue River, close to the main camp, the crews were responsible for construction at the Upper Blue and Blue Crossing campgrounds. At Blue Crossing it is still possible to see evidence of their work. The main road has been rerouted, so it no longer passes directly next to the camp area, but the steps and a stone bench at the entrance are still there, tucked out of the way. The "Adirondack style" camp shelters are there also. The Forest Service has given them a facelift since the CCC days, replacing rotten logs and putting on new roofs, but they look much the same as they did in the 1930s. The Forest Service added another nice touch when it installed interpretive signs drawing attention to the fine work of the CCC in the area.

The Blue camp was winter headquarters for Company 842. The elevation—fifty-eight hundred feet—meant that cold and snow were rou-

Eugene Gaddy at Blue campground, 1999, next to one of the "Adirondack style" shelters put up by the CCC crews from Blue camp F-03-A. The Forest Service has replaced rotted wood and refurbished the roof, but the overall look of the shelter remains true to the original CCC work design and location. Photo by author.

tine for the men. How bad could it get? Lt. Elmer E. Huber, the camp second in command, recalled that the brakes in his car froze whenever he got them wet fording the river and then parked his car. The best way to thaw them out was to get a pan of hot water and throw it against the wheels, then jump in the car and get it running before the brakes froze up again.[6]

Many things have changed at Blue since the CCC days. The old bridges have been rebuilt. FR 281 down by the Blue River has been rerouted in places to avoid river flooding. In the old days the road was closer to the river and the camp was east of the road. The modern road now bisects the camp location at Johnson Canyon. The elementary school at Blue sits in the middle of what was once Blue camp. Little remains of the old site. All of the CCC buildings are gone. The concrete slab that was once the garage area remains on the west side of the road across from the school. Beyond that, nothing of the main camp is left.

(F-04-A) NO LOCAL NAME

This camp opened on 27 May 1933, making it one of the first to open in Arizona. It is one of only two CCC forestry camps in the state (the other is located in southeastern Arizona) that official records do not

CCC camp F-04-A. This photo is labeled Jackson Springs, but the official camp name is open to question; Camp Lawton has also been suggested. Courtesy Apache-Sitgreaves National Forests.

identify with a proper name, although local sources at Alpine point to one possibility.[7] It is not uncommon for official records of the very early camps to be missing or incomplete, and such is apparently the case with F-04-A. Even the exact location of this camp is open to speculation. A camp at Jackson Springs just a few miles southeast of Alpine may have been the site of F-04-A.[8] A site just south of Alpine that was used by the Forest Service as a work center in the 1960s is another possible location.

We do know that a company of CCC men was at work in the forest around Alpine. Within two months of the camp's opening, officials at the main camp had sent the men out to five side camps—temporary camps located close to the work site—the most side locations on the national forests in either Arizona or New Mexico at the time. These men did a lot of high-altitude work. CCC crews built fire lookout towers near the KP Cienega campground on State Highway 191 and on Escudilla Mountain (see appendix 2). Two other side camps, totaling thirty-five men, were assigned to the high country doing fence work and campground construction near Hannagan Meadow.[9] Another project was the Stone Creek Road (FR 275); its completion rated a panoramic photograph of the job crew.[10]

The men who worked at the camp were from Company 847, organized in Texas and top-heavy with enrollees from the Lone Star State. Fewer than forty in the company were Arizonans. In later years, shifts in enrollment patterns gave the majority to Oklahoma boys. Not until 1939, when the company was working grazing projects at Arlington, near the town of Buckeye in the central part of the state, did Arizona boys outnumber all others.

In October 1933, after one summer of intense work, the camp was officially abandoned and never reopened. After leaving Alpine, the company went to work at Grand Canyon National Park and never returned to the White Mountains.

HART CANYON (F-21-A)

Hart Canyon was the first camp set up on the Sitgreaves National Forest; the first work company reported in late May 1933. The setting was beautiful. There was plenty of flat bottomland for the tents, and the canyon had gently slopping sides that protected the site from high winds. As usual, the sleeping tents for the men went up first, followed by a few frame buildings before the first month was out.

The CCC boys at this location were all from Arizona. Most were from the southern part of the state and got their initial training and conditioning at Fort Huachuca, Arizona. They were organized as Company 823 exactly one month after Congress authorized the CCC program, making

Hart Canyon camp F-21-A kitchen mess area, June 1933. Courtesy Apache-Sitgreaves National Forests.

them perhaps the earliest Arizona unit to participate in the national relief experiment. By mid-June they were fully settled in at the new camp.
Once there, the company filled out its two-hundred-man roster with
men from Maricopa County (Phoenix). The unit included twelve African Americans, the most in any of the new camps along the Rim and
White Mountains that first year. After spending a pleasant summer in
the woods, the company left for winter camp at J. K. Ranch near Roosevelt Lake in early November 1933. They never returned to Hart Canyon. The next summer the company was assigned to Los Burros near
Pinetop.[11]

Photographs of Hart Canyon camp show it to be as comfortable and
clean as a tent camp can be, but it was still remote in the 1930s, and there
was some grumbling about that in the Los Burros camp newspaper, the
Los Burros Brays:

> After a night spent on the train and a half day over cow trails in
> a truck without a bite to eat, we reached Hart Canyon. In less
> than a weeks time we transformed it from a Hell Hole to a re-
> spectable place to live.[12]

As for the work schedule, the crews did a lot of fencing on the forest,
but much of their work dealt with road building and improvements intended to make the area more accessible for fire control. Most of the major numbered Forest Service roads in the area—including the old Rim
Road (FR 300)—show the handiwork of Company 823. The latter road
has become a popular scenic drive to recreation lakes and camp areas,
but it still serves its original purpose. The devastating Dude fire of 1990,
which destroyed large areas of timber in the rugged territory below the
Rim, was finally stopped as it came up over the top of the Rim thanks in
large part to crews and equipment that arrived at the fire via FR 300.

Hart Canyon camp was also the farthest west of the Sitgreaves Forest
camps. When the boys closed the camp after that first summer season,
the company paper described the road as "just two cow trails," making
it sound as if they had to claw their way out, even though the Indian
Gardens CCC camp near Kohl's Ranch was just a few miles south. No
records indicate that the camp was used again after the summer of 1933.
A few men from Los Burros might have used it as a side camp or travel
stop the following year, but the record ends there. The tents and few remaining frame buildings were taken down, but no one knows for sure
what happened to them.[13]

Hart Canyon itself is still very much off the beaten path, and finding any trace of the old camp is almost impossible. Logging operations in the 1950s ran roughshod over the site, and there is little to indicate that the camp was ever there. The area has since recovered from commercial logging and has reverted to the beautiful site it once was. Weekend campers now set up their tents and equipment on the old grounds without a clue that a small army of young men once worked there.

LOS BURROS (F-22-A)

Los Burros, another early camp on the Sitgreaves Forest, was first occupied by recruits from Texas on 3 June 1933. Unfortunately, their food did not come with them. The company had some nervous days in camp before the supply train arrived during their third week of occupation. That first company spent one summer season in tents at Los Burros before moving on. They left behind a very good start on rodent control on the Mogollon Plateau between Show Low and Heber and on fencing projects near Lakeside.

Company 823, the next unit to occupy the camp, stayed for several seasons of work. The company was first organized in southern Arizona and originally included a significant number of Hispanics. Already an experienced crew after other CCC jobs in the state, they arrived at Los Burros on 3 May 1934. Since leaving their winter camp near Miami, Arizona, the company had picked up new enrollees from Texas. Counting the additional new men from Globe and Miami, the roster had an almost even mix of Arizona and Texas boys.

The post office for the camp was at McNary, a lumber town located on the White Mountain Apache Indian Reservation. No alcohol was sold on the reservation, and that didn't sit well with the local timber men. Pinetop, across the line and close to the CCC camp, however, did sell liquor, and more than one CCC veteran recalled that weekend auto accidents on the road between Pinetop and McNary were common as intoxicated drivers tried to make it back home.[14]

All of the company's work assignments were on the Sitgreaves side of the forest. One major job involved rodent control. The camp newspaper of 14 July 1934 made much of the fact that a "doggie" roundup crew had been sent out to eliminate the prairie dog population on twenty thousand acres in the plateau country east of Heber near the community of Aripine. The 1934 job schedule also called for work on a stock water sup-

Los Burros camp F-22-A, June 1933. The corner of the camp boxing ring is barely visible at far left. Courtesy Marshall Wood.

ply tank near Heber, construction of sixteen fish-rearing ponds at the Pinetop hatchery (a long-term project of which the men were especially proud), water well improvement at the Lakeside Ranger Station, and a boundary fence line between the national forest at Pinetop and the White Mountain Apache Indian Reservation to the south.

A side camp was set up in mid-July 1934 to begin construction of the Pinedale Ranger Station. The CCC built an office, barn, water storage tanks, and a house for the forest ranger, complete with landscaping and fencing. That type of work was a bit different from the usual forestry jobs, but it taught the men useful skills. The 12 October 1934 camp paper reported that "crews are shingling the house, others digging ditches for pipes. . . . Many of the men are learning about construction work on this new project." They must have learned their trade well. The house, office, and barn at Pinedale are still standing and now serve as part of the Forest Service work center. The house is still being used as a ranger residence.

During their stay at Los Burros, the timber stand improvement crew of Company 823 was asked to supply peeled timber for the reconstruction of the ancient Indian pueblo of Kinishba on the Indian reservation near Fort Apache. Such a request was rare because CCC workers almost never left their assigned forest to do work on the reservation.[15]

In 1936 Los Burros was host to Company 862. The men from that unit were mostly from Texas, Oklahoma, and New Mexico, with a scattering of Arizonans. The group was well traveled, having seen duty in New Mexico and Wyoming before coming to Arizona. By the time they were assigned to Los Burros, they had already worked at the Juan Miller (F-65-A) and Three Forks (F-55-A) camps on the Apache National Forest.

When Company 862 reported for duty, the camp was starting to show its age. Los Burros was a summer camp, and the tent barracks for the men had to be taken down each winter. The canvas was in such bad shape that it was recommended that the tents be condemned after the 1936 season. Perhaps it wasn't a coincidence that the boys did their best to get duty at the one side camp in operation that season.

The side camp at Willow Springs that summer of '36 was reputed to be "one of the best, if not the best" camp in the CCC district.[16] The tents had plywood walls six feet tall, and screen doors instead of tent flaps. Fifty men (an unusually high number for a side camp) were stationed there. Contact with the outside was rare. The boys were an amazing eighty-three miles from the main camp at Los Burros. Despite the isolation, they must have enjoyed the setting. Given the opportunity for leave in Winslow, the recruits chose instead to remain at the camp. When the enrollees back at the main camp got wind of the conditions at Willow Springs, a note went into the camp suggestion box that a rotation system should be set up to allow others to spend time at the new side camp too.

Pennsylvania recruits identified as Company 3348 spent a short summer season at Los Burros in 1938. These men were part of a larger group from the Keystone State that ended up scattered all over the southwestern region. This group left Los Burros after less than four months and reported for duty at Nogales, Arizona. Six months later they were moved again, this time to Williams, Arizona.[17]

Los Burros camp was located in what is now the heart of Pinetop. The urban growth explosion that started in the 1970s has obliterated the campsite. The land was transferred to private hands and cleared to make room for the Pinetop Country Club. There is nothing left to see of the old camp.

INDIAN GARDENS (F-23-A)

Located near the banks of tranquil Tonto Creek, the Indian Gardens camp had a breathtaking view looking up at the Mogollon Rim escarpment—so beautiful, in fact, that others had been drawn to the site long before the CCC arrived. Native Americans had hunted and camped on the Tonto for hundreds of years. Pioneer homesteaders came next, among them the Kohl family, whose namesake resort still operates on the creek. In the 1920s author Zane Grey discovered the splendor of the Rim Country near Indian Gardens. Grey included a description of the Tonto Creek area in many of his bestselling books, most prominently in *Under the Tonto Rim*. He liked the area so much that he had a cabin built for himself a few miles upstream from the future Indian Gardens camp.[18] Grey brought Hollywood movie crews there on several occasions in the 1920s to film silent reels based on his wildly popular western adventure novels. The economics of the Great Depression forced the Hollywood studios to curtail shooting on location in the Rim Country in the 1930s; it was too remote and too costly. It seems a bit ironic that the government spent several thousand dollars to build and operate a camp for two hundred CCC men in this same remote area.

Indian Gardens, which opened in late May 1933, was in the very first round of camps set up in Arizona and missed being first in the state by a single day. In fact, the men arrived a couple of days before the official opening and spent the first few nights sleeping under the stars and taking their meals in the open while their camp buildings were being completed. This was brand-new Company 807, only the seventh group of men to be organized in the CCC's 8th Corps southwestern region.

Company 807 would see service at several camps in central Arizona before it was all over. Like so many others in the state, the company worked the mountain country in summer and moved south for winter jobs. At first the men spent their winters near Roosevelt Lake. In 1937 they opened the Ashdale–Cave Creek camp (F-34-A) north of Phoenix. In 1941 their winter duty took them to the Pinal Mountain camp (F-16-A) near the copper-mining town of Globe. The Pinal camp was also among the first in Arizona and was one of the few camps that remained in operation all the way to the end of the CCC program.

Shortly after Indian Gardens opened, a side camp for twenty men was established about seven miles upstream. They could have not have picked a more beautiful setting. The job site was at Horton Creek, nes-

Indian Gardens CCC camp F-23-A, looking north toward the Mogollon Rim escarpment. This undated photo may have been taken in 1934 by U.S. Forest Service supervisor F. Lee Kirby, who frequently traveled the Rim Country with his camera. Courtesy Tonto National Forest.

tled under the cliffs of the magnificent Rim. High and quiet, it was like another world. Bracken ferns, mosses, and other lush greenery not found in the open forest lined the trickle of a stream. The area is still something of a hidden treasure, even though it is easy for hikers to access. As one walks the uphill trail to the head of Horton Creek today, it is hard to imagine that CCC boys were once up there swinging shovels and axes for a net pay of five dollars a month. Their tasks included building a truck trail, erosion control, and watershed protection. Most of the work involved constructing a series of check dams on the creek intended to benefit fish and bird populations.

For the summer of 1934 the camp superintendent had contemplated constructing 750 erosion control dams, three miles of stream improvement, seventy-five fish ponds, one hundred cubic yards of flood control levees, a pipeline water system, and several smaller projects such as a recreation dam and two springs for livestock. In fact, however, the men spent a lot on time on fire duty that summer. Crews cleared thirteen hundred acres of underbrush hoping to reduce the fire danger. Even so, enrollees put in an additional 513 man-hours fighting fires, and by mid-July the water projects were less than 50 percent complete.[19]

The company also spent a lot of time on road construction east and west of Tonto Creek. To the east, the men set up a side camp in Gordon Canyon and set to work clearing a road to Pleasant Valley. Most of that work involved improving the northern end of FR 200, the Chamberlain Trail, mainly around Turkey Peak and on south toward Fisherman's Point. To the west, CCC boys worked on the road to Payson. The most time-consuming project was construction of FR 64—the Control Road. Several seasons of work were necessary to finish just the part nearest Indian Gardens. The men established several side camps as their work took them deeper into the woods. The side camp on the East Verde River was later reestablished as a main CCC camp after Indian Gardens permanently closed.

While at Indian Gardens, Company 807 was also responsible for working on the campgrounds in the area, especially those along upper Tonto Creek. They cleared ground and constructed tables and fire rings using native stone. Other stone work closer to home involved construction of flood control walls and outbuildings at the nearby Indian Gardens Ranger Station.

For more than sixty years following the end of the CCC program, the road from Kohl's Ranch to Payson ran immediately in front of the Indian Gardens camp. The site was on the south side of the highway about one quarter mile west of Kohl's Ranch. In 2004–05, highway construction shifted the road alignment of State Highway 260. Although the road was moved less than a half mile north, that was far enough to obscure a clear view of the site.

The campsite itself has changed little since the 1930s. Despite its proximity to Kohl's Ranch, the site is still managed by the Forest Service and is not subject to commercial development. Nor has the area become overgrown with trees or scarred with side roads, so the site still has the general appearance it had when the boys first arrived. The most striking evidence that remains of the camp is the flagpole base constructed of native stone by the first unit that arrived at Indian Gardens in 1933. A plaque mounted in the base acknowledges the presence of Company 807 and includes the names of several camp leaders and work supervisors. It is the only marker of its kind in the forests of the Mogollon Rim and White Mountains. Behind the flagpole is a broken concrete slab marking the spot of one of the administration buildings.

BAR X RANCH (F-24-A)

The Bar X Ranch was another of the very early camps, and it was certainly the most remote one in the Tonto National Forest. From the rail-

Company 864 at Bar X Ranch camp F-24-A, 1933. This is the only known photograph of that company at their camp below the Mogollon Rim. Courtesy Eddie Blumer.

head at Globe, it was a long truck ride north to the Salt River and then up and along the spine of the Sierra Ancha into a wilderness that sixty years earlier had been the heart of Apache Indian resistance. From the crest of the Sierra Ancha the road ran down into Pleasant Valley and the ranching town of Young—historically famous as the site of the frontier feud between the Graham and Tewksbury families in the 1880s. From Young, the CCC boys had yet another ride north to the camp itself on Haigler Creek at an elevation of just over fifty-two hundred feet.

The Bar X is something of a mystery camp because so little can be found about it in the official records. The site was used for a single summer season and then abandoned. Whereas Indian Gardens, its neighbor to the west, had semipermanent wood-frame buildings, Bar X was a tent city all the way. The closest thing to permanence there was the wood-frame sides and canvas tops on some units such as the kitchen. We know a bit more about the men who were there and the kind of projects that kept them busy.

Company 864, organized in Texas, was the only tenant at Bar X Ranch. Arizona enrollees accounted for only 35 of the 185 boys reporting at camp; the rest were Texans. The company also included ten African Americans.[20] The unit's job list that summer of 1933 included at least one big undertaking: road improvement on the Chamberlain Trail (FR 200).

The boys worked mostly on the stretch of road from Young past the camp on Haigler Creek and continuing north toward Fisherman's Point, a sharp angle in the road about three miles north of the camp. Getting the job done did not always involve sophisticated civil engineering. At one spot the crew hand-dug a ditch where the road was supposed to go. Then a small-bladed "cat" running with one track in the ditch scraped off the topsoil with its blade, creating a primitive roadway. The next year, a CCC crew from nearby Indian Gardens would tackle this same road, coming in from the north off Highway 260 via the Colcord Road. Despite the weeks, days, and hours of work put in by both the Bar X Ranch and Indian Gardens crews, the Forest Service ultimately had to finish the road after the CCC program expired.

Nowhere else along the Rim or White Mountains is there a more storied history of ranching than in Pleasant Valley near the Bar X site. Even though the days of blood feuds and frontier shootouts were more than forty years removed, it seemed logical for the CCC boys at Bar X Ranch to engage in jobs somehow connected with cowboy life. Since frontier days there had been a sheep trail that ran from the Rim Country near Heber down off the mountains toward Cave Creek and Phoenix. A section of that trail came off the Rim near OW ranch and ran through Pleasant Valley and the area worked by the CCC boys of Bar X Ranch. Work orders no longer exist, but it is known that crews from the camp on Haigler Creek built spring boxes from FR 512 (the main road into Young) on the east to the Chamberlain Trail on the west that became essential watering stops on the sheep trail to and from Phoenix.[21]

Sheepmen moved their herds from one spring to the next along the trail, but natural springs were often muddy and occasionally contaminated. To solve the problem, the boys from Bar X shored up the spring and ran a pipeline a short distance to a small concrete-lined tank called a spring box, which was capable of storing clean water. Thanks to their work, herders could count on reliable water as they moved their sheep through Pleasant Valley.

Although most of the unit's work involved erosion control on roads and watersheds near camp, the Bar X boys built a number of toilet houses for the residents of Young. Each had a concrete floor, and many of these were imprinted with the letters "CCC."[22] Also in town, the crews helped build a wall at the Pleasant Valley Ranger Station.

In November 1933 the company left Haigler Creek and moved down to the A-Cross camp in Tonto Basin near Roosevelt Lake. In 1934 the men of Company 864 went on to Phoenix, where they contributed to the development of recreation sites at South Mountain Park. The Bar X camp was abandoned and the official records on the camp's jobs and operations disappeared.

The original CCC campsite is on the east side of Haigler Creek a short distance south of the Haigler Canyon campground, on a level stretch of ground just above the floodplain of the stream. The area saw human occupation before the CCC boys arrived. Pottery shards and broken arrowheads from ancient Indian campsites can still be found up and down the creek. The land was also a pioneer ranch site before and after the CCC men were there. More recently the area has been discovered by weekend campers. Parcels of land along the creek have been subdivided and sold for summer homes.

The actual CCC campsite is on private land and is quickly being overrun by modern cabins whose owners generally have no idea that two hundred young men once lived there. It is easy to understand why the newcomers do not know about the site. Trees as well as houses have grown up and filled in much of the CCC grounds. Because it was a tent camp occupied for only a single summer, no concrete foundations or stone walkways mark the site. Yet, scattered between the modern homes one can still find old rusted cans and trash that may go back to the CCC days. Only the baseball diamonds south of the camp are still in open country and have not yet been touched by development.

EAGLE CREEK (F-48-A)

This camp was located in the lovely Eagle Creek River valley in the southwest portion of what later became the Apache National Forest. The only link to civilization was forty-five miles of twisting road leading southeast to the railhead at Clifton. The advance team of Company 2857 left the relative comfort of Petrified Forest near Holbrook in August 1935 to prepare the camp for occupation. Company 2857 was a new company put together from transfers from other units, but luckily a few of them were local experienced men (LEMs) from Safford and the Gila Valley who were familiar with the area. Later, a contingent of men joined the company from the panhandle country of Texas.

The advance team had the task of completing the camp's construction and making it livable for a crew of two hundred. A pipeline to the water tank, faucets along the main street, and rock walkways were started immediately. The bathhouse and recreation hall were finished next. Until then, the men ate out in the open and their food came off the army field ranges "mixed with plenty of sand, mud, and rain."

It is no wonder that the new rookies from Texas needed time to adjust to camp routine and deal with homesickness. Some of them never did. At the end of the enrollment period in October 1935 the company discharged more than sixty-five men. The camp paper noted that "the largest percentage were boys who just couldn't adjust themselves to camp life and didn't care for the thought of staying."[23]

The forestry work began soon after the full company arrived. The first task was to improve the road into camp. Finished in 1926, State Highway 191 (the Coronado Trail) was the best access from the camp to Clifton. It was also the only north–south state highway in eastern Arizona. The Coronado Trail was a challenging trip for one traveling from Clifton north up the narrow switchbacks to the high country near Alpine. Starting at Highway 191, graders and other heavy equipment set to work widening the road west toward Eagle Creek. Behind the machinery came men with picks, shovels, and other tools to add the finishing touches, which included rock walls to divert storm water. North of the camp along Eagle Creek, a smaller crew of CCC boys worked at Honeymoon Park building a rock dam for flood control and making improvements to the campground.

Expiration of enrollments reduced the company's strength, but the men who left were soon replaced by Arizona boys. In early 1936 the camp at Glenwood, New Mexico, was disbanded and sixty-two Texas and Oklahoma men from there were transferred to Eagle Creek. With the company now at almost full strength, the forest work shifted into high gear. The road from the Coronado Trail into camp and on north up Eagle Creek to the Honeymoon recreation area was nearing completion and included two bridges.

The benefits of the CCC's work for local residents were obvious. The company newspaper, the *Eagle's Nest*, proudly boasted on 30 March 1936 that thanks to the hardworking young men, cattlemen could truck their stock to the pens at Clifton in three hours rather than the three or four days of trail herding required before the CCC boys went to work.

Indeed, much of the CCC work in this area directly benefited the ranches and homes along Eagle Creek. Cattle range mismanagement had been responsible for past erosion in the area. The company built fencing so the Forest Service could protect the watershed and individual ranches could keep track of their cattle. In 1937 CCC crews drilled wells and constructed stock tanks to further alleviate the problem.

Flood control crews on lower Eagle Creek straightened the river channel, built a flood wall, and filled an irrigation ditch at a bad spot called Filliman Box. Together those projects made the road usable all year round and permitted residents of the area, and especially the Eagle Creek school bus, to get in and out safely. The ranchers up and down the creek showed their appreciation by organizing dances for the boys. "The dances would last until late and the boys would stay overnight. The ranch wives would give them breakfast the next morning, then they would return to camp," reported Mrs. Irene Andrews.[24]

By the summer of 1936, three side camps had been established. The Juan Miller camp (F-65-A) was a thirty-six-man road construction crew. The work on the Juan Miller Road (FR 475, going east from Coronado Trail to the Blue River) involved putting in cattle guards and working on the Juan Miller Bridge. A twenty-four-man crew was at Engineer's Spring near Rose Peak working on the road up to the tower and developing the Strayhorse recreation area near the Coronado Trail. This was a typical forest side camp because the distance to the main camp was short "as the crow flies." In fact, the route from the main camp snaked out of Eagle Creek on a dirt road, then went north and uphill on the Coronado Trail to the spring for a total distance of about forty-five miles. The work farther north at Strayhorse added another fifteen miles. The third side camp, as the company half-jokingly referred to it, consisted of the lone enrollee atop the Rose Peak fire lookout tower. He had an easy, albeit lonely, duty. The fire season that first year turned out to be light, with the main camp being called out only once.

As was the case in other forest camps, the isolation at Eagle Creek caused inconvenience, if not frustration. Going to town involved a two-hour ride "over a mountain road considered hazardous in many places." Camp officials also reported that "the very small town of Clifton is the nearest settlement, and there is little there to amuse enrollees. . . . Altogether it may be said that enrollees are not very keen for the trip." It is no wonder that few enrollees made the trip. Going to the weekend movies in Clifton meant staying overnight, and the men had to find and pay for their own accommodations. Those who decided to spend the weekend in camp had few options beyond pickup baseball games and hiking in the mountains.[25]

Despite the hard work and lack of outside entertainment, the company's first anniversary in the woods was cause for a special celebration. The recreation hall, not yet finished when the men first arrived, now had more than 350 books and fifty current magazines, plus a pool table, Ping-Pong, and other table games. The festivities that first year included a barbecue, free soda pop, and a variety of contests and games. Several hundred local people were invited to the party, and the highlight of the event was an evening dance. Musicians were hired and trucks were sent into town to bring the young ladies, "properly chaperoned," to the dance and return them later that night. The camp's newspaper, the *Eagle Forester*, reported that "a big time was had by all."[26]

When Eagle Creek closed in late 1937, some buildings were taken down and moved to a Department of Grazing camp. Other buildings were given to the Forest Service for administrative use. Eagle Creek is still ranching country, just as it was in the CCC days. The campsite is mingled with private ranchland, and even some of the local people cannot pinpoint its location.

BUFFALO CROSSING (F-54-A)

Located high in the White Mountains in the middle of the Apache National Forest, Buffalo Crossing was a typical summer camp. Mostly tents with a few semipermanent frame buildings, the camp was active for

Buffalo Crossing camp F-54-A, June 1934, while still under construction. Courtesy Apache-Sitgreaves National Forests.

more than five years—a relatively long time by CCC standards. During the winter the camp was closed and the men moved down to the Blue River to work; they returned to "The Crossing" in the early summer. Beautifully situated on the east fork of the Black River, this camp was the summer home of CCC Company 842, whose men were said to favor it over the more permanent-looking facilities at Blue.

Early summer is the fire season in the mountains of Arizona, and the Forest Service made the men of the CCC the first line of defense. That was especially true of Company 842 at Buffalo Crossing. Every man received training from forest rangers on the use of firefighting equipment, and they didn't have to wait long to use it. By early summer 1937 they had already fought fifteen fires in less than a month. The men considered that number below normal compared with the year before, when the company fought more than forty fires during June.[27] Most fires were discovered early and did not develop into runaway wildfires. Crews could usually control a moderate fire within a day or two. But with firefighting the number one priority, it was not uncommon for other work projects to be delayed at Buffalo Crossing.

Among the major work done by this camp was the ongoing construction and improvement of FR 276, the Diamond Rock Road. Several seasons were spent working on the road, campground, and fencing north of the camp. Several miles south of Buffalo Crossing, another crew was at a side camp at Hannagan Meadow improving the Coronado Trail.

In addition, the company spent at least three summers working at Big Lake and Crescent Lake. A group was sent there in 1935 to raise the dam and construct spillways. Crews were also part of a fish-stocking program at Big Lake in 1936. Two years later a side camp was established at Crescent Lake for fence and bridge work and for additional work at Big Lake. CCC boys were also active in the area putting in cattle guards on Forest Service roads.

Buffalo Crossing camp's location in the middle of the White Mountains was beautiful, but some of the men simply couldn't handle the isolation. Homesick boys from Texas deserted at a high rate.

Despite minor problems, inspection reports over the years gave Buffalo Crossing good marks. While recognizing the off-hours drawbacks, officials pointed out that "enrollees have many forms of recreation that is not available in other camps, such as fishing, and horse back riding." In later years the camp developed an excellent library and recreation room. General morale remained high, and there were no "official" complaints from enrollees about the food.[28]

Baseball and fishing in the nearby stream were the favorite off-hours activities. The east fork of the Black River was a short walk from camp. The trout fishing was excellent, and even the camp commanders couldn't resist putting a line in the water.

Long after the CCC days, the camp location was used as a Forest Service work camp. The current Buffalo Crossing primitive campground sits on the site of the old CCC and Forest Service camp.

THREE FORKS (F-55-A)

Three Forks camp was located east of Big Lake on gently sloping ground in the heart of the beautiful White Mountains. The site was protected on three sides by trees; the open side looked south onto a peaceful meadow of tall summer grass. The water supply came from the cold and sparkling creek running through the middle of camp. A more lovely and picturesque mountain location could hardly be found. The site was typically remote, but the biggest drawback to Three Forks was the weather. The high-altitude camp was strictly a short-season, summer-only work center. Winters there were impossible, and the climate was almost too cold in the summer. The men lived in stove-heated walled tents, but even in July they could not stay warm enough. The camp's commanding officer said that it was not necessary to issue summer shirts to the men who worked here. They wore winter underwear and flannel shirts and were comfortable wearing both.[29]

In the summer of 1934 the camp was home to Company 1830. This company was unusual because it was a "veterans" unit. National CCC policy included a provision that allowed veterans of the Great War (World War I) to enroll. Americans generally felt that the country owed something to those who fought in that war. Because of the dire economic conditions of the time, war veterans had been denied a promised monetary bonus from the federal government for their service to the country. Allowing veterans to participate in the CCC was one way of showing national appreciation for their wartime sacrifices and getting money to them.

When the CCC program began in 1933, the average Great War veteran was forty years old. Partly because of their age, it was logical to organize these men into companies with fellow servicemen rather than

Three Forks camp F-55-A, home to a "veterans" unit, June 1934. Courtesy Apache-Sitgreaves National Forests.

mixing them in with the younger fellows. Their camp duties and jobs were sometimes modified to adjust to their physical condition. Official reports from the highest levels of the CCC organization pronounced the veterans units a success, with soaring enrollments, and offered individual stories of how uplifting the experience had been.[30]

Three Forks had the only veterans company in the Rim–White Mountains area, and their experience didn't match the hype from Washington. The veterans didn't stay long, and they left with rather a mixed reputation. Their work foreman and army camp commanders were younger men, and there were stories that the vets didn't like working for nonveterans or men younger than they were. The seven-year-old son of a crew supervisor was certainly impressed by the vets. He later remembered the hard edge that some of these mature men had.

> Most of these men were heavy drinkers, and I remember going into the kitchen of the camp one day when several of the enlisted men were sitting and telling stories. . . . One of the men poured a water glass full of whiskey and then broke an egg into it. After looking at it for a while and jokingly offering me a drink, he turned it up and chugged the whole thing. It took me a while to get over that experience.[31]

While at Three Forks, the veterans worked on several miles of road improvement in the area and constructed more than six miles of telephone line. They also did some landscaping work at the Water Canyon Ranger Station south of Springerville. A Department of Agriculture official from the Biological Survey was on the payroll that summer of 1934, so that meant the men were working on a prairie dog extermination project too.[32]

The veterans from Company 1830 were from Arizona, Texas, Wyoming, and Oklahoma. They had begun their tour at Pima, Arizona, in the Gila River valley and moved to the high country of the Apache National Forest in May 1934. After their duty at Three Forks they moved on to Carlsbad, New Mexico, and never returned to the White Mountains. In 1935 an experienced group (Company 862) of nonveterans from Texas, Oklahoma, and New Mexico set up at Three Forks. At the end of that summer they transferred south to Juan Miller camp (F-65-A) and likewise never came back to the lovely meadow. Indeed, there is no record that Three Forks was ever occupied after those first two seasons of work. There certainly was more work to be done in that part of the forest, but camps at Buffalo Crossing (F-54-A) and Greer (F-76-A) were nearby, and it is possible that their men took over the work from the Three Forks area.

The camp was located next to FR 249 almost midway between Big Lake and Alpine; the forest road now bisects the site. Motorists traveling this popular route will see nothing of the camp from the road. As was true with most of the high-country summer camps, Three Forks was mostly a tent site easily broken down and moved when its work was done. However, a few concrete slabs remain where the administration buildings once stood.

JUAN MILLER (F-65-A)

Solid information about this camp is scarce. Informal records indicate that Juan Miller was a seasonal work station and may have been used as a side camp for the more established CCC company at Eagle Creek. Thus a note in the 15 June 1936 *Eagle's Nest* reported, "Men at the Juan Miller side camp have been employed on the Juan Miller road, finishing work started there by camp F-65-A before their departure."

The camp was very close to State Highway 191, so it seems likely that the CCC crews at Juan Miller were involved in roadwork. It would be easy for crews to work the Coronado Trail from that camp and also to drop off to either side for forest road improvement farther back in the woods. FR 475 leading down to the Blue River fits that category of work.

The campground at Juan Miller is certainly CCC work, but it is unclear which camp was responsible for its construction. It would have been convenient for the company from Eagle Creek to use the Juan Miller location to get the job done. There is a suggestion in the Eagle Creek camp newspaper that it was used as a side camp, perhaps in the same way that Company 842 on the Blue used Buffalo Crossing as a summer camp.[33]

The location of this camp is now bisected by State Highway 191. The full camp was probably on the immediate west side of the Coronado Trail north of Clifton near the junction with FR 475. In the years after the CCC, the highway was rerouted here, cutting through the old camp and leaving nothing to see.

PIVOT ROCK (F-75-A)

Pivot Rock was one of three camps set up in the western sections of the Mogollon Rim within a couple of years of one another. All three (the others being Chevalon Canyon and East Verde) were relatively close to each other. Camp supplies and material for both East Verde and Pivot Rock were offloaded at organization and supply headquarters in Flagstaff and followed the same route south into the forest, with East Verde the last stop. Pivot Rock was so far away on the edge of the Rim, though, that immediate necessities were more easily found at the small town of Pine. Each day a driver would be sent down off the edge of the Rim to pick up the company's mail. The duty was close to a full day's job for the driver, considering time spent picking up goods in town and the slow trip back up to the top.

Pivot Rock had all the common problems associated with remote CCC camps. Desertions were common. Most of the documented dishonorable discharges were due to absences without leave. During the first two seasons the camp had at least one dishonorable discharge almost every month. Even pleas directly from the camp commander often failed to keep some men in camp. The official reports called the camp "tremendously isolated."[34]

The camp's appearance reflected its isolation. The camp buildings were battered hand-me-downs from other camps. The barracks for the men were tents rated by inspectors as "good." "Good" really meant "av-

Men from Pivot Rock camp F-75-A, tending the Leroux forest nursery, 1941. Courtesy Coconino National Forest.

erage," because the "good" category was in the middle of the inspection classification. In addition, inspectors rated the 550-gallon underground gasoline storage tank as inadequate. Because tankers had to travel such a long distance to deliver gas, CCC officials thought it more economical to send 1000 gallons at a time. However, the inspectors thought it unwise to store the surplus in 50-gallon drums scattered around the camp.

Yet, there was a plus side to life at Pivot Rock. The water at camp was good (it was rated much higher than the living quarters), and fresh fruit and vegetables were available locally. The camp had the benefit of experienced leadership and technical crews, and there were very few on-the-job accidents. The camp also had a permanent medical officer and an outstanding educational program.

Pivot Rock was home to Company 863, which had a long history of service on the Coconino National Forest. Its members were among the first round of enrollees assigned to camps in 1933. Like so many other units in the Southwest, this one was organized in Texas before being assigned to duty in the Grand Canyon State. Thus, only 54 of 184 enrollees that first year were Arizonans. Their first assignment was at Double Springs (F-6-A) near Mormon Lake southeast of Flagstaff. Their winter seasons were spent in a number of camps in and around the Verde Valley.[35]

Like the nearby CCC camp on the East Verde River, Pivot Rock started as a side camp. In 1936 the main camp of Company 863 at Double Springs sent 120 enrollees to the Pivot Rock area—well over half the company strength and an unheard of number for a side camp. Their job that summer was mostly twig blight control. The men cut and burned the limbs of almost twenty thousand trees and pruned an area of more than six hundred acres. They were also called into duty as firefighters. Later that same year, their main camp at Double Springs was permanently closed.

The following summer Pivot Rock was designated a main camp. The same company came back every year, working through the final summer in 1941. Ironically, a large side camp was set up at Mormon Lake in the summer of 1940 on the site of Double Springs Camp, the company's original summer home.

Work assignments seem to have been typical of those performed by other CCC camps, although official reports are vague enough to lead to some interesting speculation. For example, one of Pivot Rock's 1940 work projects called for lookout tower construction. Baker Butte was the closest tower to the main camp, but that tower was started in 1937. The Buck Mountain tower north of Pivot Rock and south of Mormon Lake falls within Company 863's work area, but that tower went up in 1939. Perhaps the company put in some touch-up work, possibly on buildings associated with tower operations.

Public campground development was also on the work list for Pivot Rock in 1940, but exactly where the campground was located is not known. Road construction and fence work were part of the crew's duties that summer as well.

The 1940 fire season was a bad one on the Coconino Forest. By early summer lightning had started more than one hundred fires in the Long Valley district north of the Rim. Forest Service resources were quickly overwhelmed, and the boys from Pivot Rock were called to pitch in. Even CCC manpower was not enough. Forest officials took to the streets of Flagstaff, Winslow, and Jerome looking for any able-bodied men who wanted to make some money fighting fires.[36]

By 1941 Company 863's enrollment had dropped to around 150—not unusual that late in the CCC's history. Perhaps the talk of war caused some men to question their future in the program. In any case, the character of the company changed during those last years in the woods south of Flagstaff. More Arizonans joined the ranks as the out-of-state boys went home or into the armed services. When that final season came at

Pivot Rock, there was an almost fifty-fifty split between Texans and Arizona boys in the unit.[37]

The campsite itself is on top of the Mogollon Rim west of State Highway 87 on FR 616 in the Coconino National Forest. Modern campers who happen to find the site make use of the concrete slabs that were once CCC administrative building foundations, which now make level campsites for RVs. Little else remains at the site.

GREER (F-76-A)

Another of the high-country summer camps in the Apache National Forest, Greer Camp was first occupied in May 1938. The site was in a meadow close to the Benny Creek campground, just north of the present Greer town site. The few local residents called the camp the "Greer Dump" because they had dumped their garbage there in years past.[38] The main administrative buildings such as the kitchen and mess hall, education building, and infirmary were portable frame structures as specified in the standard CCC building plan. The officers and men were housed in sixteen-foot-by-sixteen-foot pyramid tents that were said to be easy to move. Built at an elevation of almost eighty-three hundred feet, Greer was one of the highest camps on the forest.

In the years following the CCC days many others discovered the idyllic setting of Greer. Summer homes and resort lodges have sprung up along the clear stream bed of the Little Colorado River. The valley has become a destination for sport fishermen, wildlife watchers, and high-country hikers. Throughout Arizona the name Greer brings to mind white puffy clouds, relaxing walks by the stream, and cool summer breezes. But there is another side to Greer.

Winter in this part of the forest can be long and cold. The winter wonderland may be heaven for today's skiers and snowmobilers, but it would not have been pleasant for outdoor workers like the CCC boys. Snow accumulations and sloppy dirt road conditions can make the roads impassable. CCC administrators and Forest Service rangers in the 1930s knew this too, and it was the common practice to officially abandon the high summer camps during the winter months. The Greer camp went through that process during the fall of 1938–39 and again the following year. Aside from the formal government paperwork, the routine was as simple as taking down the tents and trucking the men out before the snow arrived. The few frame buildings usually stayed up, making for an easier move-in the following spring. But even that effort may not have been worth it at Greer. Apparently summers there were just too short. The camp made it through only two seasons of work. The summer of 1940 was the last.

The CCC men who came to Greer had served first in the desert country of southeastern Arizona. Company 2848 was assigned to the Soil Conservation Service at Bowie, Arizona, in the early spring of 1936. From there it moved to the Noon Creek Camp (F-41-A) on the Crook National Forest near Safford. The men's first season at Greer was probably in 1939.[39] During the winter the crew moved back to the Noon Creek site.

The company had a unique addition to its rolls in 1940: the unit roster at Greer included one World War I veteran. Most of the military veterans in the CCC served together in veterans units. Many of these former soldiers quickly tired of the military-style camp routine and left the CCC service. Late in the program it was very unusual to see any veterans attached to units. But there he was, an older fellow working alongside all those youngsters along the banks of the Little Colorado at Greer in 1940.

Well-traveled civilian supervisor Tom Flanagan was at Greer for a time. He had the men cutting down and clearing dead trees in the area as a fire prevention measure. The wood was conveniently cut small enough to fit into a cabin stove, so it wasn't necessary to haul it away. The crews simply left it, and the residents picked it up and used it to heat their homes. Another job at Greer was to survey nearby Tunnel Reservoir. The use of a boat would have made the job easier, but there was none to be had. Flanagan slapped together a homemade craft, and they got the job done. After the survey was complete, the local youngsters were allowed to play with the boat for the rest of the summer.[40]

Projects benefiting recreational activities were numerous. The CCC crews built check dams on the Little Colorado River where it ran through Greer Valley. The dams gave fish a place to hide and develop. That work, plus operation of the fish nursery upstream from Greer, greatly improved the area's trout fishing. Crews also built benches, tables, and fire pits at the local campgrounds. At Sheep's Crossing near the entrance to the Mount Baldy Wilderness Area the CCC boys built a camp area plus a unique pipeline system that brought fresh spring water to the site.[41] The crews also graded roads for better access to the Greer Valley and maintained telephone service to the area.

Official records do not pinpoint the exact location of Greer camp, and no readily visible signs of it remain. Because it was there for only two short seasons of summer work, finding the site through on-the-ground inspection or artifact search would be time-consuming—if it were possible at all.

EAST VERDE (F-77-A)

East Verde was a side camp of Indian Gardens that became so convenient for work projects that it was given main camp status after Indian Gardens closed. Like so many others, this camp was far removed from headquarters. Official CCC reports hint at problems when they describe the road from Flagstaff as "good gravel road 70 miles, fair dirt road 15 miles."[42] The nearest railhead was at Flagstaff, and the company's mail came in at the small ranching community of Pine, about thirteen miles west of camp. Some reports also list Kohl's Ranch and later Payson as mail pickup sites.

The camp itself was of standard size, but unlike Chevalon, which was built at about the same time on top of the Rim, enrollee housing at East Verde was exclusively in tents. Clearly, the camp was intended only for summer duty. Six weeks after East Verde opened in September 1939, the camp was shut down and the crew moved to winter quarters at a lower altitude. They were back again in May 1940 for a full summer season in the woods.

Job assignments at CCC camps throughout the country covered a wide range of construction tasks, and East Verde had its share of different jobs. But it appears that the camp was established and strategically located for one important reason: completion of the Control Road (FR 64) below the Mogollon Rim.

The camp at Indian Gardens on the east end of the road had made significant progress in previous years, but the remaining section to Pine was not yet finished. As the boys worked their way west, construction naturally took them farther and farther from the main camp. Before Indian Gardens closed in 1937, its crew had put up a side camp on the East Verde River. Ironically, it was the same company from Indian Gardens (but not necessarily the same men) that was assigned to finish the job, working now from the new main camp on the East Verde.

Besides the road itself, crews were kept busy building bridges, including one 140-foot steel structure. The final summer of work in 1941

Washing up at the East Verde side camp, 1936. The camp was used by Company 807 from Indian Gardens as a base while constructing FR 64. Courtesy Tonto National Forest.

saw them adding four masonry bridges as well as telephone lines, two lookout buildings (not the towers), and a total of ninety miles worth of road "betterment" or improvements on existing roadways.

The camp's location along a significant river like the East Verde ensured that some jobs were water related. Five miles of stream improvements and construction of water pipelines were on the final camp project list, along with twenty acres of recreation ground development.

Of all the camps in the Rim Country and White Mountains, East Verde seems to have had the best morale. Official reports noted that the nearest railhead was at Flagstaff, almost one hundred miles away, "with little or no attractions in between," yet praised the camp in all other matters, especially camp leadership, food, and sanitation. The recreation room—so important at an isolated camp—was rated "superior." Weekly movies, more than one thousand books, seven daily newspapers, and a variety of athletic equipment provided pleasant entertainment for off-hours. Overall enrollee morale was rated excellent.[43]

The site was on the eastern side of the East Verde River a short distance north of the Control Road and northeast of the Whispering Pines residential area on the Tonto National Forest. Its site ensured a dependable water supply. The actual campsite is near the confluence with Dude Creek on just about the only level land around. Like other former CCC sites, the location has become a favorite of weekend tourists, who also know a good campsite when they see one.

It has been rumored that the East Verde site was used and altered for other purposes after the CCC days, but it is still possible to match up the old site plan with slabs of concrete, and stone-lined walkways remain in place from the seasons of use by the young men of the Civilian Conservation Corps.[44]

CHEVALON CANYON (F-78-A)

Completed in September 1939, Chevalon was one of the last CCC camps set up in the Rim Country before America's entry into World War II ended the program. It occupied ten acres of land—the standard campsite allotment. While not officially listed as having permanent buildings, the camp looked like an established community. It had the full complement of camp buildings and featured well water that was stored in two thirty-four-hundred-gallon tanks atop a thirty-foot tower. Even after almost two years of operation, camp reports said that the "buildings are in very good condition. The camp too is of the 'Superior type' spotlessly clean, well equipped, and furnished."[45] Like many CCC camps, Chevalon had an extensive network of native stone walkways and decorative landscaping. The camp was situated on the plateau overlooking Chevalon Canyon in a mixed juniper and scattered ponderosa pine forest. Sitting high above the quiet of Chevalon Creek, it offered a wide open, beautiful view of the countryside, especially looking north down into the canyon.

The men who moved into this camp were a long way from home. They were organized in Pennsylvania as Company 3346, shipped out West, and after a few work stops in between finally ended up at Chevalon. Camp inspectors recognized the isolation of the camp, but also said there was "very good cooperation here, also good mess-lunches, and these matters are the big thing in any company."[46] The Pennsylvanians

Mess hall (right) at Chevalon Canyon camp F-78-A, 1940. A network of sidewalks connects the buildings. Courtesy Charles Pflugh.

stayed until April 1941. The company was somewhat under strength in manpower, but that did not affect the quality of the work it did. Company 3804 was the next to use Chevalon camp. It too was short of manpower—143 men in a unit that should have had 200. By that time, however, six-month reenlistment opportunities were being discontinued due to the threat of war. The company served until the camp was closed a few months following the December 1941 bombing of Pearl Harbor.

As for work projects, road construction got a lot of attention. There was FR 504, involving a stretch of territory from Chevalon Canyon east toward Heber, to be finished. In between, the road had to cross several forested canyons. As crews worked east, the distance between the main camp and the work area stretched for several miles. Two side camps were set up to reduce travel time. One tent camp was in the bottom of Wildcat Canyon, with responsibility for road building in and out of that troublesome spot. Another side camp may have been located a few miles west of Wildcat on top of a ridge between other canyons.[47]

The deepest canyon crossing of all was right below the main camp in Chevalon Canyon itself. This undertaking involved building a steel bridge over Chevalon Creek, a task that extended beyond the standard six-month enlistment period for enrollees. As new men came in, they re-

Chevalon Canyon camp F-78-A, 1999. Hidden among the trees growing in the middle of the camp are remnants of the stone walkway. Photo by author.

ceived instructions and were reminded of the payoff of being assigned to such a project. The *Chevalon Echo* reported in its 1 May 1940 edition:

> [A] few lucky would be Steeljacks are going to have an opportunity of learning the trades of . . . a steel worker. This promises to be the most interesting part of the Technical Services work for some time to come.

While the primary focus was on the bridge, a separate crew began work on a telephone line to Heber as well as a connection to the remote Wallace Ranger Station west of the main CCC camp.

The men also built the Chevalon Crossing campground just down the hill from the main camp. The campground is still there. The juniper wood picnic tables the CCC boys constructed lasted until 1997, when Forest Service crews updated the facilities and replaced them with rubber-coated metal tables.

Road-building crews also worked on Forest Service roads heading into the woods south of camp, such as the work project on FR 169 near Deer Lake that connects Old Rim Road with the northern reaches of the Sitgreaves Forest. Another noteworthy project in that direction was the building of the "Dutch Joe" fire lookout tower. The all-wood tower included a "tower cabin" and a two-room house at the base of the structure. The integrity of the wood tower became questionable over time, and the structure was built on private land, so the tower was taken down by the Forest Service in the early 1990s.

In the last year of occupation at Chevalon, crews put in ten additional miles of telephone line, completed fencing along the forest's north boundary, built four impound dams, and worked on other smaller projects of trail construction. Additional work involved rodent control and timber stand improvement (tree thinning, etc).[48]

No buildings remain at Chevalon, but evidence of the camp is clearly visible. Most noticeable are the stone-lined sidewalks, building foundation outlines, and the concrete foundation slabs near the center of the camp. The garage and maintenance areas are south of the main buildings and include remnants of timbered loading ramps and work areas. What is left of the camp is close to FRS 504 and 169. Since the days of the CCC, hunters and weekend campers have altered the area with off-road vehicle travel and scattered fire rings. In addition, the site was used as a summer field camp for university archaeology students in the 1970s, and some alterations may have been made to the site at that time. The walkways and foundations have been clearly linked to the Chevalon camp, however, and enough remains of the camp to impart the flavor of what an active CCC camp of two hundred young men must have been like at the height of its working life.

Chapter 3

The Early Days at Los Burros: Marshall Wood

By the late spring of 1933, many young American men had heard of the CCC program but didn't really know what it was. The idea sounded good, and the prospects were intriguing. There was the promise of a job and certainly some hard work ahead, but there was also the possibility of an exciting adventure—perhaps the one every young man dreams about. The CCC offered a young man the chance to get away from home and explore the country—and to be paid while he was doing it.

Marshall Wood and his Texas buddies wanted to be among the first to take part in the adventure, so they hurried to the recruiting station at Fort Worth. From there it was on to San Antonio, and before long they were on the train to Fort Bliss near El Paso, a training and orientation base for new enrollees. At this early stage of the program, no one knew for sure what kind of physical training was necessary. Marshall and his fellow Texans seem to have been simply waved through the process. "We had no special training before we left for Arizona, even though it was a military type operation," Wood later wrote (undated letter).

On 3 June 1933, after "a long twisting train ride to the jump off point for F-22-A, Los Burros Camp" (Wood letter, undated), Company 898 arrived by truck at the CCC campsite. The boys got out and looked around. They were the first to arrive on the scene. There was nothing there but a small clearing and a sea of giant hundred-year-old ponderosa pines stretching out forever. In fact, civilization was not really that far away. The camp was only a couple of miles from Pinetop in the Sitgreaves National Forest. Still, there wasn't much of a town there in the 1930s. The only real town of any size was McNary, a few more miles south across the boundary of the White Mountain Apache Indian Reservation.

O. J. Hendricksen, an enrollee who served at Los Burros four years after Marshall and his buddies were there, remembered McNary as a busy lumber town whose sawmills were "going full blast." Pinetop was closer, but if they could get trucks to take them, McNary was the destination of choice for CCC boys looking for fun, because it had a movie theater.[1]

The Mogollon Rim and the White Mountains were indeed remote locations. CCC campsites were intended to be close to work areas, and most were thus located off the main roads. Of all the camps, only Los Burros was within even moderate walking distance of a town. In the early days, camp commanders and administrators did not always plunge immediately into conservation work projects. Oftentimes the first project for many CCC boys reporting for duty was to improve the road in and out of the new camp so supplies could be delivered.

The food supply line into Los Burros was a problem. Marshall recalled that difficulties began shortly after they arrived to set up camp:

> Food was adequate for the first five days or so. After that, things got difficult. I think the supply organization must have forgotten where we were. (Wood letter, undated)

Things would get worse for Marshall and Company 898 before they got better. In the meantime, they had to set up a new camp.

Being a part of a CCC company essentially meant camping out in the woods. Opening a new camp was not unlike setting up a modern tent site for a multifamily outing. Spacing, drainage, and shade had to be considered. Vehicles had to be backed up to the site. Cooperation was necessary to put up the tents. The men had to move sleeping gear and other personal items into the tents and keep those items separate from those of their bunkmates. If the unit was staying for an extended time, a little clearing and landscaping around the tent were nice. As modern campers do today, the CCC boys had to secure firewood for the cool evenings and remember where the latrine was located.

Marshall's first night in the forest at Los Burros was a rather rude awakening to camp life:

> That first night they gave us a canvas cot, two wool blankets and a mattress cover and told us to fill the cover with pine needles because we would be sleeping out in the open. Many of us didn't

find time to gather pine needles before bedtime, and I soon discovered my error. I awoke during the night and began looking for anything I could put in that mattress cover—clothes or anything else. The cold had come right up through the ground and the half empty mattress, and was very uncomfortable. The next morning we found a covering of ice in the water buckets left out for face washing. That was in June. (Wood letter, undated)

In the early days of the program, especially in the national forests, the men lived in walled tents that could sleep up to seven enrollees. Construction of frame lumber buildings began as soon as the tents were up. The first were usually a mess hall, bath house, recreation hall, and perhaps the canteen. Even after those buildings were in, though, it was most common for the men to remain in tents and sleep on cots.

Marshall recalled that

the first few weeks were the worst, but the first few days were pleasant and eventful. Of course we were in tents during those early days. There were no buildings, except the cook shed. We were busy improving the camp with such nice features as a permanent latrine, and lava cinder streets. We built the mess hall of bark slab lumber from the Cady sawmill in McNary, but when we were done, there were cracks between the boards that you could throw a rock through. We did build one other permanent building. That was the camp canteen where razor blades, toothpaste, and other personal items were sold. (Wood letter, undated)

The food situation at Los Burros and the other camps in those struggling early days left something to be desired. As the CCC camps became more established, the system used to provide food to them got better. The overall national plan called for three meals a day, with the noontime meal usually served at the job site. Unless an enrollee volunteered for the job, the army officers would simply appoint someone to be the camp cook. That arrangement did not turn out as badly as one might imagine. There were some complaints about the food, of course, but most of the men didn't blame the individual cooks for its poor quality. Indeed, even the official government inspection reports were kind to them. Pivot Rock camp on the Mogollon Rim north of Pine reported inadequate mess conditions, but the space on the report form asking

The entrance gate at Los Burros CCC camp F-22-A, July 1933, one month after the camp opened. White sign on right reads: "Civilian Conservation Corps. Camp F-22-A. Co. 898." Courtesy Apache-Sitgreaves National Forests.

Los Burros camp F-22-A, 1933. The medical tent is at the head of the company "street." Courtesy Marshall Wood.

about experienced and properly trained cooks simply said, "young, but doing OK."

Menus were carefully prepared, reviewed by the camp commander, and published for general perusal. The boys seldom wanted for complete meals even at the most remote locations. For example, the 1934 official report of the summer tent camp at Three Forks near Big Lake recorded the menu for a typical work day as follows:

Breakfast: bacon and eggs, oatmeal, cold cereal, milk and coffee.

Lunch: Swiss fried steak, gravy, baked corn, peas, bread, black-berry pie, coffee.

Dinner: pork and beans, stewed tomatoes, cornbread, apple pie, milk, and coffee.[2]

The commanders at the Blue camp on the Apache Forest took great pride in serving meat at each of the daily meals. Not all camps were that fortunate. Eagle Creek near Clifton had problems with its mess for several months after the camp began operating. The menu of 13 October 1935 did not include a single meat item. The dining highlight for that evening was baked spinach and creamed carrots. The inadequate mess conditions at Pivot Rock camp were at least partly responsible for the dismissal of the camp commander in 1941.[3]

For the most part, CCC meals were varied and nutritious. Almost never was a meal item repeated two days in a row. Most of the men ate better in the CCC, in fact, than they would have at home. In the midst of the Great Depression, many of them went home heavier and stronger than they were when they first joined, in spite of the pick-and-shovel forest work they did all week long.

Marshall Wood and Company 898 were not so fortunate during those first few weeks at the new camp:

The first mess hall at Los Burros camp F-22-A. Hastily constructed in the summer of 1933, the room was primitive and drafty. The man seated at right is a U.S. Forest Service employee. Courtesy Marshall Wood.

The company "street" at Los Burros camp F-22-A, summer 1933. The two men at far right are camp commanders Captain Runge and Captain Walker. Courtesy Marshall Wood.

> When we left El Paso we were given burlap bags full of bread. This was intended to hold us over till the camp was properly supplied. But it took three weeks for the supplies to catch up to us at the camp. In the meantime, the bread got terribly old and hard. We even had to resort to boiling beef bones to make a type of beef gravy broth. By the second week our supplies were down to beans, coffee, flour, and the bread from El Paso. By this time it was so hard and dry that a cleaver was required to chop it up into serving size. There must have been about 260 men in camp and I'll bet half of them had diarrhea and were always at the latrine. Of course, that was one of the first things we built at the camp. The story went around camp that our military camp officers, Capt. E. C. Runge, our commanding officer, and Capt. D. M. Walker scoured the nearby towns and with their own funds purchased canned goods, eggs, potatoes and other such foodstuffs as were available to tide us over. (Wood letter, undated)

Discipline and order at the camps often depended on the character and temperament of the commanding officer. In many cases the isolation of the camp was also a consideration in how much military protocol was applied. Captain Runge was well liked by the men, and Marshall was thankful that the isolation at Los Burros translated into a relaxed atmosphere around camp:

We had very little contact with the military people. Most of them were reserve officers and I believe they thought of a CCC command as something of a demotion. We didn't have to stand at attention, salute, and all that stuff. They were content to lay back and let things happen. The Forest Service supervisors were the ones that really ran things. There were eleven or twelve of them at our camp and they were the ones who did most of the supervising work. They were a great bunch. (Wood letter, undated)

The men working in the woods did not always return to the main camp at the end of the day. Besides the main camp there were also smaller temporary work camps. These side camps—also called spike or fly camps—were located closer to specific work areas and saved time and manpower by keeping the men and their equipment in the field. This was especially useful on road and bridge construction jobs. Generally, each of the main camps in Arizona and New Mexico had from one to four side camps set up during a six-month enrollment period.[4] Since the camps were temporary work sites (they were rarely used for more than two months) the men most often lived in tents, and the number of them working at the site rarely exceeded thirty. The normally reliable camp newspapers are vague about their locations, but the work that was done

Saturday morning at Los Burros, October 1933. In this photo taken in front of the company canteen, Marshall Wood is in the front row, fourth from the left; the man at far right is a Forest Service employee. Courtesy Marshall Wood.

Marshall Wood at the rodent control side camp at Clay Springs, 1933. Courtesy Marshall Wood.

at them was not much different from that done by men assigned to jobs closer to the main camp.

Service at a side camp might seem like lonely and undesirable duty, but CCC alumni often talk about the joy of being assigned to jobs away from the main camp. Enrollees at a side camp were most often under the command of a Forest Service work supervisor, which the men generally preferred to working under an army officer back at the main camp. Without the army looking over their shoulders, rules and discipline could be conveniently overlooked. A cook was assigned to the side camp, too, so the men ate as well as or better than they did at the main camp. The boys still worked hard, but duty at a side camp seemed somehow more casual and fun.

Perhaps typical of duty at a side camp is Marshall's recollection of his time on the Mogollon Rim east of Show Low, far from the main camp:

> I was fortunate to be assigned to an eight man fly camp [near Clay Springs]. We had an experienced camp cook [Dennis Flake of Snowflake] who was an expert in such delights as "bean hole"—beans cooked with molasses and salt pork in a syrup bucket buried overnight in the coals. He made us fruit pies and fluffy biscuits baked in a Dutch oven and plenty of fresh eggs

Prairie dog extermination near Clay Springs, 1933. Marshall Wood is at far right. Courtesy Marshall Wood.

and local meats. We ate good at that camp. We rarely got back to the main camp at Los Burros except for payday.

We were out there a week or ten days at a time. We were under the direction of the Biological Survey. They were separate from the army or the Forest Service. Our job out there was rodent control. The control work was on government grazing lands near Show Low, Snowflake, Heber, Vernon, Concho, and St. Johns. I feel bad about it now, but we were there to eliminate the prairie dogs. I guess there are not too may around these days. Back then we were sent out in a field and six of us would form a line about twenty-five feet apart. We would then walk zigzag back and forth to a meeting point farther along the field. As we walked we would bait the prairie dog village with plain oats. Two or three days later the boss would walk the field and check to see if the prairie dogs had eaten the oats. Then later we would walk the field again and put out poisoned oats. I remember we mixed it in bathtub size containers. We mixed the oats with molasses and strychnine; at least I think it was strychnine. We turned it with shovels, like mixing concrete. After we put it out in the field, we would go out and see the dead animals. Once in awhile we would see a dead coyote that had eaten the poison oats too.

One of the interesting things about being out at Clay Springs was that the prairie dog field sometimes extended from government land onto private land, and it was hard to treat just one part, so we eliminated the prairie dogs on the private land as well. That often resulted in a fresh home-cooked meal from the grateful rancher. Another benefit was that while we were there, we met the Shumway family. They had a vacant house on their property, so we got to take our sleeping bags in there and stay.

It didn't matter if you were assigned to the side camps or not, you still had to come into the main camp to get paid. We only got to keep five dollars, and the rest we sent back home. (Wood letter, undated)

The prairie dog project turned out to be a big job. After Marshall and his company left the mountains, a new company assigned to Los Burros in 1934 continued the extermination assignment farther west toward the tiny community of Aripine. The "doggie" death count in that year was estimated in the tens of thousands.

The White Mountains of eastern Arizona were formed millions of years ago as part of a huge volcano field. Los Burros camp made good use of the volcanic soil and cinders in camp construction and later as part of the camp's forest projects. Wood recalled:

Fencing the public campground at Lakeside, 1933. The Los Burros fence-cutting crew takes a break to show off their work. Marshall Wood is at far right. Courtesy Marshall Wood.

We did a lot of different types of work at Los Burros. We cleaned up along the side of the road. We helped in telephone construction, and we built a lot of fire trails. We also built a fence completely around the Lakeside Community Park. I didn't go, but a few of our guys were involved in fighting a fire west of Lakeside. Another project I remember very well was when we went out to the country where the volcano mounds were. We used a tempered steel rod and we would drive it into the side of the hill. Then we would put some explosives in there and blow up that section. What we had left was fine cinders and we used it in road work around the area. (Wood letter, undated)

Transferring to a winter camp would be looked on as a bother by later CCC enrollees, but for Marshall his friends from the early days of the program, winter camp meant cozy barracks and a welcome break from the primitive conditions at the Los Burros tent camp. He recalled that

snow started falling in mid-October, and on November 15, 1933, we packed up and moved south to our winter quarters at Camp F-45-A. For some unknown reason the camp was called Airport, located three miles west of Miami, Arizona. There we enjoyed the comforts of regular barracks, very pleasant after six months of tent life. Our major project there was erosion control. . . . The winter climate was delightful, and being able to speak a little Spanish, I found the townspeople very hospitable. (Wood letter, undated)

Like so many of the young men who would come later, Marshall left the CCC service with a strong understanding of how much the experience had contributed to his personal development:

I have some very good memories of my nine months enrollment. I came out thirty-five pounds heavier, mostly muscle, and [with] a respect for hard work. Following my discharge on March 31, 1934, I returned to Wichita Falls, Texas, and eventually migrated to Virginia where I worked for forty-one years on the Chesapeake and Potomac Telephone Company. I have had many occasions to think back and thank God for my experience in the CCC. (Wood letter, undated)

Chapter 4

Time Away from the Job

The CCC camps were more than work centers. They were little towns that the young men thought of as home. In most cases a social community would begin to develop shortly after they arrived at a new camp. After working side by side in the forest, it was natural for the boys to form friendships that carried over to their free time. Some of the young men organized themselves for off-duty entertainment. They participated in athletic contests like boxing, running, and team sports. Some men used their off-hours to go hiking or fishing in nearby streams. Others enjoyed photography as a hobby, giving us unique pictures of camp life and work. In some cases, enrollee snapshots are the only photographic evidence of what the camps looked like.

Trips away from camp were a treat for young men looking for new adventures beyond their work. Once or twice a year the White Mountain camps would put together sightseeing motor tours to the Painted Desert, Meteor Crater, Grand Canyon, and other typical tourist destinations of northern Arizona. Led by their education adviser, the boys of Company 807 left their summer camp near Payson and went up to the Zane Grey cabin on Tonto Creek. From their winter camp near Roosevelt Lake, the same company received guided tours of the ancient Indian ruins of Tonto National Monument.

Charlie Pflugh recalled such trips as his best memories of CCC life away from his Chevalon Canyon camp:

> One aspect of my CCC life with F-78-A was the generosity of
> my foreman, Francis Bealey. Normally boys would sign up for
> six months at a time, and those who signed up for another six
> months were invited by Francis to take a trip to the Grand Can-

yon, Painted Desert, Meteor Crater, and Petrified Forest. Francis drove his car and we came up with some money to help out. We also paid fifty cents for four nights lodging. If the room had two beds, then it was almost totally free. Food was cheap, but even so, Francis came up with a few extra dollars. It was the most awesome trip of my life. It was a fantastic opportunity to see the beauty of Arizona on just a few dollars. It was a priceless experience. (Pflugh letter, 4 November 1999)

Marshall Wood, who served at Los Burros in the White Mountains, remembered the special plans the boys made on paydays:

On those days, I remember the Mess Sergeant always coming around trying to organize a poker game. There wasn't much else to do for fun. Pinetop didn't have much to offer, so some of the guys got rides to McNary. Once, some of us went down to the Indian Fair on the Apache reservation and got our pictures taken with the natives. (Wood letter, undated)

The highlight of Bill Dean's recreation experiences in the CCC had a Hollywood connection. In the 1920s, popular author Zane Grey used the central mountains of Arizona as a backdrop for several of his best-selling western novels. Later, he insisted that the movie versions of his books be filmed on location in the Rim Country. Although Grey became disillusioned with the studios in the late 1920s and left Arizona for good in 1929, Hollywood continued to use the Rim Country for location shooting. The most convenient route for production crews and movie stars was to board the train in southern California and get off in Flagstaff, Arizona. Fine hotels, good food, and a direct rail connection made Flagstaff the film headquarters for shooting Arizona westerns during the Depression years. Bill Dean's CCC camp was less than four miles from Flagstaff, and he remembered some exciting times there:

Back in those days many Hollywood "B" movies of the cowboy genre were filmed nearby and our cowboy heroes of the day were sometimes accessible for autographs. What a thrill! Actors that most people never heard of now were there—Tom Mix, Ken Maynard, Buck Jones, etc. I was in dreamland. (Dean letter, 20 April 2001)

Sunday church services were a part of CCC camp life too. Clergy from nearby communities were contracted to go to many of the camps,

K. O. Smith and Ed Jamison show off trout from the east fork of the Black River near Buffalo Crossing camp F-54-A, 1938. Courtesy Eugene Gaddy.

and even to side camps, on a set schedule of weekend visits. Attendance at services was optional, of course, but there is evidence that enrollee turnout was rather good.[1] At the Blue camp, three Catholic and two Protestant meetings were held each month, and reports indicate that the services were "well attended." In addition to the Protestant and Catholic services, the "veterans" camp at Three Forks had two enrollees who were "licensed preachers," and they conducted their own services each week.[2]

Shortly after the camp at Chevalon opened in 1939, a religious welcoming committee came calling. The visitors, the camp newspaper said, "belong to the Church of Later Day Saints, but their services [for the enrollees] are non denominational." The Saints stayed after the service and presented a lecture and discussion of "Ancient America." Such double duty was typical of the clergy. In other camps clergymen set up musical programs, delivered films, and visited the sick in the camp infirmary.[3]

At remote camps, it was not always possible or convenient for services to come to the enrollees, so camp commanders made other arrangements. Company 3804 at Chevalon was 85 percent Catholic, and CCC trucks, normally idle on the weekends, were made available to drive the men to Winslow for Mass. Similar arrangements were made for the boys at Indian Gardens to attend alternating Protestant and Catholic services in Payson.[4]

Off-hours around camp also provided an opportunity to engage in good-natured mischief. Jokes and pranks were a part of life in the CCC.

Every camp had its share of would-be comedians, but oftentimes the perpetrators remained anonymous. Charlie Pflugh remembered how it was at Chevalon Canyon:

> Most every camp had someone who goofed off, but I think we had very few. Every barracks at our camp had its share of pranksters who would store objects of all kinds in your bed, or move your bed to a different location and put it where you would fall over it coming in at night after lights out. I got hit a number of times but I took it in good style. After I became a supply steward, I could even the score if I had wanted to, but I never did. (Pflugh letter, 4 November 1999)

The young men's desire to get away from camp for a short time played perfectly into the hands of company jokesters. At Buffalo Crossing in 1936, the camp was under quarantine for two cases of measles. The 15 June issue of the camp newspaper, the *Blue Buffalo*, reported a rumor that a breakout was in the works. A truck was ready to go, bound for the good times in Springerville. The boys put on their "glad rags" and waited. Sure enough, the truck came in, the revelers climbed aboard, and off they went. To their dismay, the party boys were simply driven around the camp and deposited back at the starting point.

Enrollee snapshot of Buffalo Crossing CCC camp f-54-a showing tent sleeping quarters (probably after 1935). Courtesy National Association of Civilian Conservation Corps Alumni (NACCCA) Museum, St. Louis, Mo.

White River Indian Fair on the Fort Apache Indian Reservation, 1933. Note Marshall Wood (wearing hat) under the sign, center left. Courtesy Marshall Wood.

Boredom or curiosity sometimes led the boys to do a little exploring around camp. Every hike had the potential to turn into an adventure. Chance encounters with wildlife, twisted ankles, or simply getting caught out in bad weather were among the possibilities. What happened to a young enrollee at Bonita Canyon camp in southeastern Arizona, however, seemed particularly amusing. A local newspaper reported that while hiking with friends in the rocky country around camp:

> One of the group tried to climb the rock and when part way up decided it was impossible for him to go either up or down. His companions, taking advantage of his plight, refused to help him down until he promised to buy beer for them all on their return to camp—which promise was faithfully carried out.[5]

Social contacts with the neighboring towns were also a part of life in the CCC, and it appears that most townspeople looked forward to the interactions. Winslow's civic leaders invited the boys from Chevalon Canyon to the town's Labor Day parade in 1940, and the enrollees responded by sending half the camp's population, including their four-man "Hillbilly Band of Company 3346." In 1933 enrollees from the Bar X Ranch camp near Young took part in the town's rodeo competition.

Other camps held open houses and invited townspeople out to the site to mix with the enrollees. At the Blue camp, Richard Thim recalled that the boys prepared a pit barbecue dinner for any resident of Springerville who cared to visit.[6]

Dances were a universal means of promoting interaction between the camp boys and the local girls. Occasionally, dances were held at the camps, with general and informal invitations sent out to the young ladies of the town, usually by word of mouth. Although the townspeople must have been a bit leery of allowing their daughters to mix with strangers, both sides eagerly anticipated the events as a relief from the isolated existence. Ranchers on the Blue River even invited CCC boys to dances that the locals had organized for themselves.

A much more common practice was to load a truck with enrollees and drive to the nearest town for weekend entertainment. The sight of dozens of eager young men descending on their town could hardly have pleased the local elders, but on the whole there was no great cause for

An unidentified enrollee from Chevalon Canyon camp
F-78-A in dress uniform, ready for church services or a trip into town, 1940. Courtesy Charles Pflugh.

concern. A few incidents did take place, but they generally did not turn most citizens against the CCC boys.

Indeed, many of the towns formed a social partnership with the camps and included the young men in community activities. Good community relations paid off well for the enrollees at Chevalon Canyon. The 1 April 1939 issue of the *Chevalon Echo* reported that the generous merchants of nearby Winslow had purchased baseball uniforms for the camp team.

The Fourth of July 1933 was a holiday like no other in the town of Young. The Bar X Ranch CCC camp north of town was probably the most isolated camp on the Tonto National Forest. Young was (and some say still is) one of the most isolated towns in Arizona. Yet on that day, Young held the most ethnically diverse Fourth of July in its history. The local folks were the best of those who had survived good times and bad in the unpredictable cattle-ranching business. Many traced their roots to Texas, and most had been raised on stories of the shoot-'em-up 1880s range war from old-timers who claimed they could remember the days of hostile gunfire in Young.

Also present at that Fourth of July celebration were Apache Indians from the reservation town of Cibecue, a long and rugged ride across the broken forest country stretching eastward from Young. They too had heard stories from their elders about the old days, stories of fighting the whites and hiding out in the mountains around Young fifty years before.

Added to the mix were the 185 CCC men from the Bar X Ranch camp. The Texans in the group must have talked about home with locals who had a Lone Star connection. For the Arizona enrollees it must have been like coming home for a picnic. It truly was a homecoming for Ernest and Marvin Cline, because the Bar X Ranch camp was just a few miles from the brothers' family home in Pleasant Valley.

Among the enrollees who came to town on that Fourth were ten African Americans. Many of the folks in town, especially the youngsters, had never seen a black person, and they gazed on the men with wonder and curiosity. The young men were talked into joining the boxing contests that day as well, and it seems certain that wagers were made on which young black man would be left standing at the end of the final round.[7]

Back at camp there were other opportunities for the less rambunctious enrollees. Each camp had a library room, often a tastefully and appropriately decorated area for a relaxing read. At camps that operated for several seasons, more than four hundred books might be available. The room also became a sort of meeting area for relaxed conversation, a place to temporarily get away from the close confinement of barracks living. Magazines and local newspapers were usually laid out, and enrollees took a special interest in what was happening back home. The 21 September 1934 edition of the Los Burros camp paper noted that "the San Angelo [Texas] boys chipped in to have the *S.A. Standard Times,* their home town paper, sent to them as a group in order that they may know what is going on 'way back home.' "

The library at Pivot Rock camp north of Pine held more than a thousand books and more than sixty-four different kinds of magazines. It also subscribed to three Arizona newspapers and two from Texas. Hunger for news made current events the most popular course at Blue camp in the winter of 1935. For those camps unable to build an adequate library collection, the national CCC office developed a "traveling library" that made the rounds with a selected list of general-interest books and current magazines. Most popular among the boys were detective novels and works of fictional western history.[8]

The dominant off-hours recreation activity at camp was sports. Teams were organized for several different activities, with boxing and basketball being quite popular. At Los Burros near Pinetop, the first arrivals, still living in tents, found time to construct a boxing ring almost in the center of camp. But the greatest common denominator among all of the camps on the Mogollon Rim, White Mountains, and perhaps all of Arizona was baseball. The Phoenix District went so far as to organize district-wide tournaments whose finalists were mentioned in the official annual report.[9]

Enrollees always seemed to find enough level land near camp to build a ball diamond, and nearly every camp had its own team complete with uniforms and nickname. The boys of Company 842 were the Blue Buffaloes, a name that recognized their split duty between two camps. The Blue Buffaloes built two fields, one at their winter quarters on the Blue River and another at their summer camp at Buffalo Crossing. The boys at Bar X Ranch built two fields at the same camp. Their isolation at Haigler Creek occasionally forced them to chose up sides and play each other. At most camps, however, weekend games were scheduled against teams from neighboring camps and nearby towns. The boys from Chevalon Canyon camp, for example, set up a contest with the Winslow High School team—and lost. No matter. Every camp's newspaper bragged about its

The recreation hall at Blue camp F-03-A, the scene of lively card games, pool, and loud conversation, 1936. Courtesy E. E. Huber.

team and included glowing coverage complete with box scores, even in defeat.

Almost all camps had another thing in common as well—the wild nature of the surrounding country. The wilderness gave rise to stories of wildlife encounters and other adventures in the woods. Charlie Pflugh remembered that:

> wildlife was plentiful throughout Chevalon Canyon. You always had to keep your eyes open. On Sunday afternoons, I used to take a walk in the woods with a buddy to see what we could see. I was hardly ever disappointed. There were times when things became a little dangerous. One night very late when the boys were asleep, a guard walking his rounds on our campsite was surprised by a mountain lion looking for food near the mess hall. The CCC boy froze, and after a few minutes the mountain lion left. Had the boy run, he could have been killed or badly injured. I don't remember his name but I do know the camp was very much alive after that episode.
>
> Joe Begani, our hut leader, once killed a timber rattlesnake under the steps of our barracks. That was too close for me, so I was on the lookout after that. Later he killed a huge king snake out on the job and made a belt out of it. I felt a little sad about that. I guess snakes have to fight for territory too. (Pflugh letter, 4 November 1999)

The Blue Buffaloes baseball team, 1938–39. The blue buffalo on the players' uniforms denotes the dual CCC camps (Blue and Buffalo Crossing) that the company occupied during the year. Courtesy Eugene Gaddy.

As a staffer for the camp newspaper Charlie was always on the look-out for a story. The ones he was most interested in were not about work or projects. The boys wanted to read about the camp gossip. Charlie did not consider himself a gossip columnist, but he did notice what was going on around him:

> We really looked forward to our weekend breaks. Saturday meant it was time to clean the barracks, which included sweeping, mopping, and cleaning windows. This was also a fun day in the afternoon when all the cleaning was done. The boys played a variety of sports which livened up the camp atmosphere a lot. On Saturday night a group of boys had passes to go to Winslow for a night on the town. Some of them had girlfriends in town and came back with all kinds of stories to tell the rest of us. A truck would take everyone back to camp that night and if you missed it you definitely were in a lot of trouble. Camp F-78-A had a monthly newsletter called *Chevalon Echo,* and as one of the staff members on the paper, I would contribute various items. The paper was popular and provided lots of comments on items close to the boys. We joked about the girlfriends, but names didn't get into the paper. It was all in good fun. (Pflugh letter, 4 November 1999)

Undoubtedly there were thousands of "all in good fun" incidents at CCC camps across the nation. Friendships sometimes formed as a result of those comic incidents. Learning to socialize with others was part of the maturing process for the young men, and friendships could also make life more agreeable. For example, it didn't take long for the men to join forces to put together a weekend routine. Enrollee Gene Gaddy from Blue Camp explained how transportation into town could be arranged:

> We would pay the Forest Service guy a dollar each to drive us to Alpine or Springerville for the dance. He would then wait for us and drive us back to camp afterward. Sometimes there would be seven or eight of us going, so the driver picked up a good bit of money. Nobody ever bothered us in town and I don't recall any fights, but I suppose the local boys didn't appreciate us too much.[10]

Jokes, pranks, and confrontations with the local residents were to be expected, and there is little in the official record to suggest that camp commanders thought them serious enough to warrant disciplinary action.[11] In all likelihood the camp authorities never found out about the more innocent pratfalls. It also seems certain that commanders understood the young men's need to get away from work and have fun, even if that caused occasional friction with the locals.

Richard Thim, who served at Blue camp, recalled an incident that ruffled the feathers of the local community and would have been hard to keep from camp authorities:

> There wasn't much to do around camp on your off-hours. We spent a lot of time hiking and taking pictures. After awhile we had seen most everything and looked forward to going into town. Sometimes we could get away on a weekend. One time we got a ride into Springerville for the Saturday evening dance. You know how things are when a group of guys gets together to have fun. One of them said that he could get some brandy. Someone else suggested we get a room.
>
> We had a plan. You could get a room for two for $1.50. After two people signed in, all five of us planned to sneak in and stay there. There was a sheriff in town we called "Hook" because he had one arm. He happened to see us later that night standing around in back of the dance building. He must have known

something because he began to chase us. One of our guys was twenty-one, so I don't know why that one ran, but the sheriff caught two of our guys and put them in jail. A short time later he came to our room and wanted to know if we had anything to do with it. "No, no, we didn't know anything."

It turned out that one of the boys they caught was a local kid. The kid called his dad in Eager to come and get him. The next morning, the father showed up with a sad and disappointed look and said, "Son, I'm forty-five years old and I have never been in jail." With that, the boy burst out crying, grabbing the bars, and begging to be let out. I don't remember what happened next, but somehow a deal was worked out and the sheriff let them go and we all made our way back to camp wondering how we were going to explain it all. I guess that is one example why the people in Springerville were sometimes not overjoyed to see us in town. (Thim interview, 30 October 1999)

There is no mention of the incident in the official camp records or newspaper, and no further action was taken against any of the boys, so luck must have been on Richard's side.

Chapter 5

Payson and Company 807

Bonds of friendship formed through common experiences and adventures became almost routine in the CCC. Less likely was the long-term bond between a CCC unit and the local community. There were, of course, economic ties between nearly all the camps and the nearby towns. They depended on each other in order to get through the tough times. Transactions for food items, building materials, and mechanical services are just three examples of how the towns and camps could help each other. But that relationship was short-lived. The camps completed work, moved on, and left the town to wonder what happened. Of course, most CCC camps and work projects were in remote locations, and the local folks rarely saw the completed projects and didn't interact much with the men.

A few of the boys might come into town on the weekends to blow off a little steam, but that was the extent of their contact. Even then, the commotion usually lasted only a few months. The camp would relocate and the community would return to its sleepy ways. Only a very few towns in the West were able to experience the social and economic impact of the program for nearly the full life of the CCC. The ranching and lumber community of Payson, Arizona, was one of those towns.

In 1933 it was an all-day trip on a long, bumpy dirt road from anywhere to get to Payson. Originally called Union Park because of its open grazing meadows, the mile-high town was in the middle of ideal ranching country. Its location on the edge of the huge pine forest covering the Mogollon Rim gave Payson the potential to become the hub of lumbering activity in central Arizona as well. It was just waiting to happen. A few improvement projects to open up the country were all that was needed. Fortunately for Payson, for eight years during the darkest days of the Great Depression, one company of CCC enrollees was at work nearby helping to push the town's development forward.

Payson and the ranchers of northern Gila County near the rim had a special relationship with the boys of Company 807. From the beginning at the Indian Gardens camp (F-23-A) in 1933 to the end of the CCC program in 1942, the men of Company 807 worked on projects in the Tonto National Forest and around Payson—a rarity in a CCC system that kept crews moving to job sites and camps all over the Southwest. Camps and companies came and went all over the Rim Country and White Mountains, but things were different around Payson. The CCC camp at Indian Gardens (F-23-A) was about fifteen miles east of Payson, and when it was officially abandoned in 1937, a new camp established on the East Verde River north of town finished out the run of the CCC.

Even though the young men served their entire CCC enrollment around Payson, Company 807 was not a bunch of hometown boys. The unit had been organized in Texas, with a small group of Arizonans thrown in to fill out the roster. Of the almost two hundred young men who reported for duty at Indian Gardens in those early days, only thirty-eight were from the Grand Canyon State. Men came and went in later years, but the Texans maintained the advantage.

In small ways, the camp and the town helped each other in good times and bad. When the Ford Motor Sales baseball team from Globe couldn't make it to Payson for the game against the camp team, the Payson team hurriedly got together to take its place. The Indian Gardens team beat the Payson boys, but the camp players were nonetheless grateful that they had not made the long ride into town for nothing. The camp newspaper later commended the Payson team for being "great sports all through the game, even though they were unprepared for a game" that day.[1]

A few weeks later, a man (not a CCC enrollee) was killed when he fell out of a truck a few miles south of town. Officials at Indian Gardens graciously arranged to send the camp ambulance to Payson, and then on to Phoenix so the deceased would have the most dignified transportation available to his final resting place.

The crew working at Indian Gardens in the summer of 1934 was in most ways a typical CCC unit. The average age for the enrollees was a little over twenty-one. Of ninety-two surveyed that season, sixty-seven had less than a high school education. But they were all eager to learn. The camp education adviser spent a week at the beginning of the summer talking to enrollees and Forest Service staff to determine which topics the boys would like to see taught as part of the camp's education program. More than eighteen subjects were suggested, with the most popular being truck and Caterpillar driving, book keeping, English, forestry, and guitar. In the end, the number of class enrollments exceeded 180. Furthermore, the enrollees themselves helped the education program along by serving as instructors. It turned out that there were more enrollee-directed classes than army or Forest Service–taught classes combined. The education adviser, R. C. Stevenson, reserved Tuesdays and Fridays for special tutoring for those who needed the help. He also adjusted class times so as not to conflict with the normal work schedule of the camp.[2]

Melvin Lorenzen spent forty-six months around Payson as an enrollee and later as an army and Forest Service employee working for the CCC. By the time he was through, Melvin had been a part of several big projects that would have an important impact on the future of Payson:

> Around May 1, 1934, the company moved to Indian Gardens for the summer (having spent the winter in the desert country of Tonto Basin). One fly camp was set up at Gordon Canyon . . . and I started with ten men to clean the right-of-way to Pleasant Valley so that the road crew could construct a road for fire control. This road has prevented many fires from becoming dangerous because it enables men to be sent into the area quickly.[3]

The resulting Colcord Road is still used as a fire access and is still an exciting below-the-Rim journey to Pleasant Valley and the town of Young.

Also in 1934, work crews went east and west from Indian Gardens to tackle roadway improvements. Those working westward got to spend time on the Control Road (FR 64), which also became an important fire access and later a recreation route into the rough but beautiful country north of Payson and below the Mogollon Rim. Other crews were assigned to the road that ran from Kohl's Ranch (near the main camp) to Payson. That tough stretch was "straightened and gravelled, much to its improvement."[4] Later, that route was also improved to the east and became State Highway 260 leading to the heart of the forest above the Rim.

Ultimately, Company 807's major road and campground projects opened up Payson and the Rim Country to a flood of recreational use that has overtaken lumber and even ranching as the lifeblood of the community.

Every summer the camp settled into a pattern. Almost every day a driver would be sent to town to pick up mail or hardware odds and ends related to job assignments. Melvin recalled:

> The work at Indian Gardens that summer [1935] was chiefly fish and stream improvement, building pond for feeding fish that had been hatched elsewhere and shipped to Indian Gardens to rearing ponds, where they were properly fed and cared for otherwise.[5]

Also in 1935 a bonding of sorts took place between enrollees and the citizens of Payson when a side camp was established in town—a rarity among the forest camps—although there is no record of how everyone got along. The twenty-man crew was using the town as a base while building a telephone line south to the Roosevelt Lake area. Melvin was on that project too, working during the winter season in Tonto Basin south of Payson.

Winter duty for Company 807 was within fifty miles of town. In the early years the company reported to A-Cross camp near Roosevelt Lake. The Tonto Basin–Payson telephone line that Melvin worked on was started in the desert country by Company 807. He learned a new skill then:

> It was during this period that I received an acetylene torch and I became a welder because of my previous experience outside the camp. I am certain that at least three fourths of the cross-arm braces on these poles were welded on by myself.[6]

Main Street in Payson, the focus for ranching and timber in remote Gila County, 1927. Courtesy Northern Gila County Historical Society, Inc.

Members of Company 807 at Chamberlain side camp, 1934. The solid building suggests this camp was operational for a longer period than was usual of side camps in the Rim Country. Courtesy Tonto National Forest.

He got a lot of experience on telephone work. By the time the project was finished Melvin must have felt that he was part owner of the line. After his welding jobs were completed he was sent back to the shop to make telephone poles for the Tonto Basin–Payson line. When the crew moved back to Indian Gardens for the 1935 summer season, the men at the Payson side camp finished the telephone job.

The Indian Gardens camp closed for good after the 1937 summer season, capping a four-year run for the men of Company 807. If part of the mission of the CCC was to prepare men for jobs in the real world, then Melvin Lorenzen definitely had a leg up on the competition. He had worked as a rock layer on erosion control projects, as a telephone lineman, and as a blacksmith's assistant. He was a welder and an ambulance driver. His driving experience led to bigger things even before he left the service of the CCC:

> I was driving for the Caterpillar crew and we graded the road from Pleasant Valley to Indian Gardens. . . . Upon arrival at Indian Gardens I was sent with the cat crew to the East Verde fly camp where I remained all summer doing road work.[7]

In October 1937 the Forest Service salvaged the buildings at Indian Gardens for other administrative uses on the forest. By that time the company had moved to winter quarters at Ashdale camp (F-34-A) near Seven Springs north of Cave Creek, Arizona. That would be their winter home for the rest of the CCC program. While the company's tour of summer duty at Indian Gardens was finished, their association with the Payson area was not.

The Control Road from Pine to the East Verde was still a rough two-track slice through the woods. A new camp, East Verde (F-77-A), was needed to finish the job. Records show that the camp was set up sometime in the fall of 1939, although Company 807 may have used the site as a side camp the previous summer.[8] In any event, the company came back to East Verde every summer until the end of the CCC program. Various records show the company's post office pickup at either Pine or Kohl's Ranch. In 1941, during the final summer of work, the company came home one last time when Payson was officially designated as the post office site for the East Verde camp.[9]

Since Payson was the closest town of any real size, it seems likely that the company continued its tradition of off-hours social mixing there. There were very few native Arizona boys to show them around town. Even late into the CCC experience, the company remained overwhelmingly Texan. At the end of the 1940 summer season, in fact, there were only four Arizonans on a roster that totaled 184 enrollees.[10]

The final year at East Verde was one of pride mixed with apprehension for the boys of Company 807. By 1941 the company's strength had shrunk to 149. Talk of war was everywhere. Camp commanders organized three classes for national defense training. Yet morale was excellent, and work projects were rated "very good, considering the low strength of the company." Camp commander Hoyt Reames and subordinate commander Aubrey Davis had less than six months of command experience between them, but both had worked their way to the top after starting as clerks in the CCC three years earlier. The men liked them, and official reports to Washington called Reames "very capable . . . with good personnel throughout the camp."[11]

East Verde was officially abandoned on 7 November 1941, exactly one month prior to the bombing of Pearl Harbor. Company 807 was allowed to finish out the winter season at Pinal Mountain camp near Globe before going off to war in 1942.

Chapter 6

Happily Ever After on the Blue: Eugene Gaddy

Eugene Gaddy was a young man of twenty when he joined the CCC in April 1938. His adventure began when he met the other Texas rookies at Fort Sam Houston near San Antonio. They boarded a train and headed west. The last stop on the line was Silver City, New Mexico. There to greet them were army officers who divided them up (almost at random, it seemed) and assigned them to the several camps in the area. Gene was told he would be serving with Company 842 at camp F-03-A. Those numbers didn't mean much to Gene and the other Texans at the time, of course, but he soon found out that he was now part of one of the longest-serving CCC companies on the Apache National Forest.

The Blue camp (F-03-A) had been up and running since June 1933, and its wood-frame buildings were as permanent looking as facilities ever were in the CCC. The camp was considered to be winter quarters even though it was at an elevation of about fifty-eight hundred feet. Those living in the Blue River country could expect cold and a fair amount of snowfall, and Mother Nature did not disappoint. Still, the weather never held up work projects for very long. By the time Gene got there the company had already completed a number of major campground and road projects up and down the Blue River.

Gene began his tour at Blue as a carpenter, but he advanced quickly, and by the end of his first enlistment period he had moved on to supervisory duties. The CCC enlistment limit was one year, but Gene liked the life. After he had served the CCC maximum, Gene was hired as a project assistant and thus saw three years of service at Blue camp.

The company's routine was well established long before Gene arrived.

It was standard procedure that during the summer months the company would move higher into the White Mountains to a place called Buffalo Crossing. Although Buffalo Crossing was officially listed as a main camp (F-54-A), not a side or temporary location, at its elevation of almost seventy-five hundred feet it was strictly a summer camp. There were a few frame buildings, but the men slept in big, round tents, six men to a unit. At the end of the summer the tents were taken down and stored, and the men moved back to the Blue camp. Company 842 returned to Buffalo Crossing every summer. Gene recalled:

> A local rancher was hired to look after the vacated camps (both at Blue and Buffalo Crossing) after the men had left for the season, but you didn't need to worry much about Buffalo Crossing. Being high up in the mountains, even if you could get there, you would be up to your eyeballs in snow. (Gaddy interview, 10 October 1999)

During the Monday-through-Friday work week, the CCC boys were most often under the jurisdiction of U.S. Forest Service employees, who took them to the job sites and told them what needed to be done. The boys also received special training from the rangers. Instructions on firefighting came in handy. "We must have fought a million forest fires. At least it seemed like it," remembered Gene. Every man in camp knew how to use basic firefighting tools.

The work assigned to the men was similar to that done in other CCC camps. Building bridges over the Blue River, installing culverts, and making campground improvements were common work orders. Sometimes the jobs took them far from the main camp. After Gene became a sergeant in the company he had to send a four-man detail more than twenty miles away to Greer, high in the White Mountains, to help with campground cleanup. Gene also remembered the remote side camp at KP Cienega in the rugged mountains southwest of camp, high above the Blue River in the pines along the twisting Coronado Trail (State Highway 191). The CCC crew constructed tables and toilet buildings at the campground. While improvements have been made since the 1930s, the campground is still there, compliments of the boys from Company 842.

Forest Service officials had the men during the work week, but the camp's army officers often put them to work on Saturdays till noon. The most common tasks were gathering firewood for the coming week and general camp cleanup. After that, the men had the rest of the weekend

Eugene Gaddy at Buffalo Crossing camp F-54-A, 1938.
"No. 8" identifies the tent barracks. Courtesy Eugene Gaddy.

to themselves. Gene especially remembered the good times when the enrollees were off duty. His favorite pastime was photography. "I had a little camera," he recalled, "and I just went out around camp taking pictures." Perhaps the greatest number of surviving photographs from life at Buffalo Crossing and Blue camps are those in Gene Gaddy's family collection.

When Gene arrived for duty in 1938, the company was almost equally divided between Texans and Arizona men. The latter group included many Hispanics from the Globe and Safford areas. There were also a few men from Oklahoma who were serving out their enlistments and going home. Every month some would be discharged and rookies would take their place, but the ethnic mix stayed roughly the same.

After Gene had risen to a leadership position in the camp, he became responsible for leading work crews in the field. The September 1939 issue of the *Blue Buffalo,* the camp newspaper, reported that Gene and his crew were busy putting in cattle guards on a forest road northeast of Big Lake and hoping to complete the project before the company relocated to the Blue for the winter. Out on the job or back in camp, Gene always looked out for his men. It was Gene who carried complaints and concerns from the young men to the camp commander. Few were of a serious nature. The poor quality of the food at dinnertime was a typical gripe.

Gene also looked after the rookies. Once, he was asked to meet several new recruits arriving by train at Holbrook and escort them to Blue camp. Like an army sergeant, it was up to Gene to protect the new guys from bad influences:

> We had gotten a late start and had to spend the night at the Adamana CCC camp [near Petrified Forest National Monument]. There were some fellows working there from Pennsylvania. The language around camp was just rude and the men were rowdy. I couldn't wait to get my guys out of there and back to the Blue. (Gaddy interview, 10 October 1999)

The camp education adviser at Blue and Buffalo Crossing offered a number of evening classes for the men. The classes focused on personal improvement in two major areas of study: vocational training such as forestry, truck operations, and explosives; and traditional school subjects such as geometry, spelling, and journalism. "You know, there were a lot of guys who couldn't read or write," recalled Gene, "and those seemed to be the classes that got the most attention."

The education adviser also looked after the camp library and arranged the occasional evening movies—and they weren't forest training films either, but full-length movies from Hollywood. "When the local folks heard about our movie nights," Gene remembered, "they would come over to our camp with their families and join us" (Gaddy interview, 10 October 1999).

Among the most anticipated events for the off-duty men were the weekend dances. Once in a while these dances were held just up the road from the camp at Blue. The enrollees loved the convenience—no need to pay a driver for the long trip to and from Springerville; entertainment was free and within walking distance. Gene remembered it well:

> We would sometimes have dances at the Joy Hunting Lodge down along the Blue River. That was the building behind the post office. It was funny that the post office and bar were in the same stone building. The Lodge was about a mile and a half from camp, and I remember many times walking along the road back to camp in the dark. (Gaddy interview, 10 October 1999)

One drawback about dances held on the Blue was the lack of female dance partners. Betty Marks was the daughter of a forest ranger and had lived on the Blue all her life. Far from being intimidated, she "felt kind of honored to get all that attention" (Gaddy interview, 10 October 1999).

Gene and Betty noticed each other during the CCC days and struck up a romantic friendship. Living the dream of many a lonely young man away from home, Gene courted Betty and later married her. They left the area to find jobs in the copper industry at Morenci, Arizona, but the Blue River country of the White Mountains called them back. They returned for their retirement to a house just a mile or so from the old Blue CCC camp.[1]

Chapter 7

The Camp Newspaper

Perhaps the single most unifying element of CCC life, aside from the forest work itself, was the camp newspaper. Almost all of the main camps of the Mogollon Rim and White Mountains had one. It became a source of pride—proof that the camp was a special community. More than any of the official reports coming from the government, the camp papers offer the best perspective of life in the CCC. Each camp's paper was written by the enrollees themselves using camp typewriters and was printed at the campsite. The volunteer staff—an editor and as many as eight or nine helpers—tried to put out an issue every month, but deadlines were not taken very seriously.

The general goal of the paper was to highlight special events, personal stories, and elements of camp life that some of the men might have missed during the course of a normal work week. Updates on forest projects and jobs completed rated secondary coverage and rarely made page one. Also, a rehash of national, international, and local news was not part of the paper's mission. The men had access in their library to regular newspapers and could keep track of outside events using those sources. The camp papers didn't try to mimic regular newspapers in style and format, either.

The editors decided what would go into the publication, and they tried to print things the men would find interesting—camp gossip and items about recreation or education, for example. There is also evidence that they cared very much about how the paper looked. No photographs were reprinted in the papers, probably because the technical means to do so were not available at the camp. Instead, hand-drawn illustrations by the men were used to enhance the look of the paper. There was almost always someone in the camp with a special gift who didn't mind having it seen in print.

Although there was never any direct competition between camp publications, each company sought the best illustrator for its paper. Camp advertisements encouraged enrollees to come forward and show off their skills. A comparison of camp newspapers from the White Mountains–Rim Country CCC camps shows that some editors were more desperate for drawings than others. It appeared to be no coincidence that a camp that had an artistically talented enrollee would also have a liberally illustrated newspaper.

Besides the cover, each segment of the paper (sports, forest news, etc.) usually had an appropriate drawing or heading of some kind. Some papers showcased artistic talent with a comics page that featured cartoon likenesses of officers, supervisors, and barracks buddies.[1]

The finished editions looked more like small school notebooks than modern city newspapers. Each paper had a soft-cover title page (sometimes on colored paper) that included artwork that was most often linked to a special topic or holiday. Thus, the February issue might show a drawing of Abraham Lincoln, and the July issue usually had a flag or patriotic banner on the cover. If a special dance was being held that month at camp, the cover page might show a couple dancing. The publication was free to the men, with a five-cent charge for additional copies. Some camp editors printed an address label on the back so that the paper could be folded, stamped, and mailed to the folks back home. Company 2857 at Eagle Creek in 1937 printed part of the paper in Spanish so the Hispanic enrollees could more easily keep their friends and relatives informed.

Most of the camp papers had the same general format. First, there was usually a one-page message from the commanding officer, often an "editorial" welcoming newcomers, discussing morale, or encouraging the enrollees to better themselves through education classes. On occasion the camp doctor would add comments about treatment of minor ailments and general health information for the men.

Personal tidbits about the enrollees usually followed. Most common were remarks about the fellows whose CCC enlistments had expired, often mentioning future prospects back home and offering a "well done" for past service. A list of new enrollees who had just reported to camp was usually included as well. It was almost standard to print their home-

The comics page from the *Chevalon Echo,* 1940. Courtesy Charles Pflugh.

towns and suggest that the rookies read the paper for advice on how to get along in camp and live up to the company traditions.[2]

Starved for news to fill the paper's pages, the camp editors would print almost anything that was not part of the usual routine. Among the more heartwarming of these articles was an item published by the Eagle Creek (F-48-A) camp's *Eagle's Nest* in 1935. Enrollee Dwayne Blair had gotten a telegram telling him that his father was ill and the family needed him back home, but Dwayne had no money to make the trip. The other men at camp learned about his problem and wanted to help, but they had no money either. They went to their sergeant, Raymond Booker, who secured a loan to make sure that Dwayne could get back home to his father.

But getting one's name in the paper was not always reason for congratulations. Consider this 1940 incident from Chevalon Canyon on the Sitgreaves National Forest published in the *Chevalon Echo* under the heading "News Flashes":

> Walter F. Vickry a rookie that was lost on our forest a few weeks ago is in very good health at the present time. This is to warn the rest of you men of the danger of getting lost in the forest out here in Arizona. If you fellows would like to see what the forest is like, please go with some older enrollee. Anyone who is doubtful about getting lost out here, just talk to Vickry and he will tell you the results of his almost drastic experience.[3]

Even though all enrollees at Chevalon were warned not to wander away from the work site, this young man got separated from his crew several miles from the main camp. Search parties went out into the woods that day and the next, without luck. They were about to go out again on the third day when the crews saw a figure in the distance. As the figure drew closer, they recognized their friend and rushed out to greet him. It was a glad and grateful reunion.

The *Blue Buffalo* celebrates Thanksgiving 1939 with this fanciful cover art. Courtesy Center for Research Libraries, Chicago.

Another story from the Chevalon paper must have embarrassed its subject:

> Frank Burchik was attempting to park his truck in his garage.
> He failed to notice that the garage was already occupied by Mr.
> Gilbert's pick up [Gilbert was a work supervisor]. The pick up
> was the worse for the incident.[4]

No mention was made of the conversation Frank later had with Mr. Gilbert or the penalty for damaging the boss's truck.

Slackers sometimes found themselves featured in the camp paper. Out at the job site it was the supervisor or LEM who instructed the men, and it was up to him to make sure the enrollees performed their duties. Those who did not fully contribute got a lecture on teamwork and proper work ethic. Such conversations were often overheard by other enrollees, and soon the word spread to the rest of the crew. Worse still, the newspaper spread the news to everyone else in camp as it lampooned them as "gold bricks."

Playful but sometimes hurtful banter back and forth on the job site between the enrollees must have been common, yet it rarely made the camp newspaper. The 12 January 1937 issue of the *A-Cross Angelus,* the

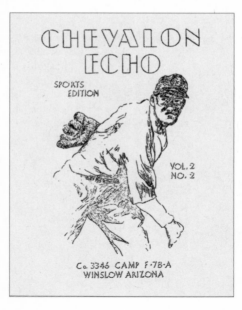

Newspaper cover art from an unknown enrollee at Chevalon Canyon camp, 1940. Courtesy Center for Research Libraries, Chicago.

winter edition of the Indian Gardens unit, made an exception when it remarked,

> This company was originally organized about half Texas and half Arizona. Now it is about half Oklahoma. . . . [T]here has been a lot of wise cracking about the alleged low grade of people in whatever state you did not happen to come from. . . . Any state has good men, better men, and also sad to relate some not so good. A fellow cannot very well help where he came from. . . . [W]here he is going is the main consideration.

Judging from the amount of space devoted to the subject—sometimes more than one page—camp sports were of special interest to enrollees. Boxing, basketball, barracks versus barracks softball, and even Ping-Pong tournaments were regularly reported. But baseball was always the sport of premier interest. The *Blue Buffalo* printed a box score for many of the games. Building a ball diamond on the rocky top of Chevalon Canyon must have been as challenging as a road project, but it was worth every drop of sweat when

> we played the Heber Lumberjacks. . . . [T]his was the first game that the boys have played on the camp ball field. F-78-A had a field day, winning by the score of 19–4.[5]

Games were played against local town teams as well as against other CCC camps. The names of those town teams sometimes reflected the ethnic character of their players. The team of the Los Burros CCC camp, which was close to the White Mountain Indian Reservation and the mountain community of McNary, played the McNary Latins, the St. Johns Spanish Team, the White River Indians, and the McNary White Team.[6] Racial segregation was not unusual in 1930s America, but the CCC team at Los Burros seems to have been well integrated.

Baseball was so popular that the subject got space in the paper even when nothing happened. The *Indian Garden's Idyls* of Company 807 noted that the team's game could not be played because all of the trucks normally used to take the players into town had been "dispatched on business". The editors lamented that "Payson fans are eager and anxious to meet our boys, who are fully anxious to try their swagger on the diamond."[7]

Another popular page of the camp paper dealt with the education

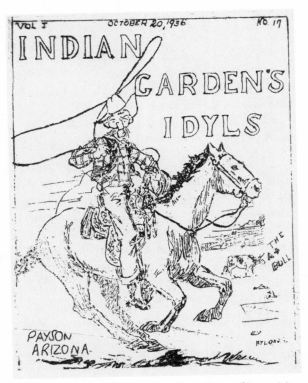

This *Indian Garden's Idyls* cover reflects the ranching spirit and livelihood of the Payson area. Courtesy Center for Research Libraries, Chicago.

program. Everyone knew that training for the men (both academic and vocational) was a central goal of the CCC program. Class offerings were routinely published in the paper, and they usually noted whether the instructor was the camp education adviser, a Forest Service employee, or perhaps a knowledgeable enrollee or LEM. The education adviser often included notes about class content and attendance.[8]

The Forest Service page of the paper explained the status of ongoing projects and outlined the kind of work planned for the future. Since there were a number of projects going on at the same time, the news helped to keep the men informed about the jobs of which they were not a part. The men could get this information piecemeal through camp conversations, of course, but those working at the side camps might go weeks or longer before they returned to the main camp. During that time there was almost no way of knowing what was going on elsewhere on the forest. The page helped them to keep track of what their buddies were doing at other job sites and at the same time lessened the impact of camp rumors. The *Eagle's Nest* from Camp F-48-A and the *Indian Garden's Idyls* of F-23-A regularly reserved a portion of the paper for reports of events from the side camps. The Forest Service page was also used to acknowledge good work on completed projects—sometimes with an added bonus. The *Blue Buffalo* of 18 October 1937, for instance, noted that "twenty-seven enrollees of Co. 842 were guests at a dinner given at the Diamond Rock Lodge in commemoration of the completion of Highway 276 to that Lodge. The enrollees attending were the ones who have a hand in the construction of the road."

Finally, each paper usually reserved space for company history, information about visitors to camp, staff promotions, medical reports of accidents or illnesses, updated camp rosters, and jokes. Various jokes submitted by the men would sometimes take up a full page. Almost none would qualify as comedy classics. Most were of the "you had to be there" category. Many were work related, like this one from the 8 September 1936 *Indian Garden's Idyls*:

> P.Mc: "What did that truck driver say when you ordered him off the road?"
> Shorty Cox: "Shall I leave out the swear words?"
> P.Mc: "Yes"
> Shorty: "He didn't say anything."

Camp editors also went looking for slightly more uplifting material. Occasionally a fellow could be persuaded to come forward with a few lines of work-related verse, and thus was born the poetry corner. While there seem to have been no Carl Sandburgs or Emily Dickinsons in the CCC camps, a surprising number of the verses from the men were insightful in their own workaday way. The 15 December 1937 edition of *Blue Buffalo* featured this offering from enrollee Felipe Villanueva:

> *There is a Camp in Arizona*
>
> There's a camp in Arizona
> By the banks of the river Blue
> Where I will spend the winter;
> and perhaps my whole life through,

Mother Nature has all done it
she has carved with mighty hand
All that is in Arizona
Which is made of rock and sand

All in all it's just a dandy
And I think it's just a fine
Everything it's just a beauty
In this famous camp of mine

So I'll stay in the tree army
In this camp I love so true
In that camp in Arizona
Near the banks of the river Blue

Another message comes through as one reads the camp papers to-day—pride in the men and their accomplishments. The papers encouraged enrollees to excel and often reminded the rookies that the camp had high standards. The 26 October 1935 edition of the *Eagle's Nest* of Company 2857 told its readers about the progress the men had made on a brand-new camp:

> From a group of struggling eaglets, it [the camp] has developed into a small city of full fledged Eagles, who fear no task but respect all tasks. The place which was formerly an unsightly, rocky hillside is now a bustling camp. . . . New boys coming have an unwritten heritage to uphold. . . . [M]ay it be ever so with the Company, showing improvement . . . even though it seems perfection has been attained.

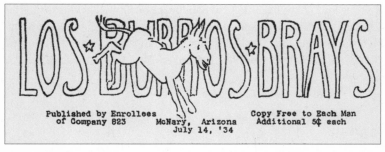

Published by Enrollees
of Company 823   McNary, Arizona   Copy Free to Each Man
                        July 14, '34   Additional 5¢ each

Banner from the Los Burros camp paper, *Los Burros Brays,* 1934. Courtesy Center for Research Libraries, Chicago.

The 1 April 1940 *Chevalon Echo* boasted about the company moving into a newer facility at Chevalon Canyon: "The camp now occupies one of the most modern and complete portable camps and at the last inspection by the District Commander was rated as Superior." The *Los Burros Brays* of Company 823 near Pinetop led off the 31 August 1934 edition with the comment that many in the camp "fail to realize the high rating that this camp holds in the estimation of the members of the Forest Service Supervisor's office and in the Regional Forest Office."

Company 3348 from Pennsylvania was briefly assigned to Los Burros before moving on to Nogales. The company's August 1939 newspaper, *The Dreamer*, bragged that "the stay in McNary was short but long enough that Company 3348 became the best company in the Arizona District." The paper conveniently failed to offer inspection reports, evaluations, or other documentation to support this overblown claim.

Above all else, the camp paper was a reminder that the boys were part of a larger group. It offered a way for them to reach beyond their tent mates and to understand that the whole company was working toward a common goal. Far better than any government document, the newspaper articles indicate how groups of two hundred men lived and worked in isolation in the woods. Aside from the remembrances of the old-timers themselves, the camp papers are the real record of the CCC boys and how they dealt with growing up away from home.

Chapter 8

A Pennsylvania Boy in
Arizona: Charles Pflugh

Charlie Pflugh would have to catch up with the other Pennsylvania boys. A large group of them had already gone west about two years before. They were Company 3346, and like Charlie, they saw the trip as a grand adventure. Eager to get away from hometown life and experience something new, the men of Company 3346 crowded around the bulletin board at the Pennsylvania Reception Center pointing to a map of Arizona and wondering what their destination town, Williams, would be like. They were among five thousand Pennsylvania men who were being transferred from the Army 3rd Corps area to the 8th Corps in the Southwest. Their group was the last company to leave the CCC Reception Center at Tobyhanna, Pennsylvania. As such, the boys got a big sendoff at the train station from various dignitaries, including John McEntee, the future national director of the Civilian Conservation Corps.

On 2 August 1938 the train carrying the men of Company 3346 pulled into the station at Williams. Dignitaries were also waiting for them there. The mayor, the chief of police, and the Williams High School Band welcomed the young men. Speeches were made and greetings exchanged; then the men boarded trucks and headed nine miles south to their summer home at J. D. Dam (F-28-A). They didn't stay long. Soon it was on to their winter camp at Noon Creek (F-41-A) near Safford, in eastern Arizona.

In the summer of 1939 the company made the move to Chevalon Canyon (F-78-A) in the plateau and canyon country of the Sitgreaves National Forest. The camp was on a promontory overlooking the canyon and a lovely stream below, and the enrollees enjoyed a panoramic view of wide-open blue sky and green landscape in all directions. The forest of juniper and ponderosa pine was quiet and remote. There was a good dirt road north to Winslow, but travel south into the woods was an adventure. Heading in that direction, the elevation gradually increased. Dense stands of ponderosa and mixed conifers closed in around the road. There were no towns. Wildlife was everywhere. Finally, thirty-five miles south of camp, there was the escarpment of the Mogollon Rim. That natural cliff barrier stopped travel. From the edge one could look down nearly two thousand feet to the seemingly endless green carpet of trees and the mountains beyond. Travel east or west from Chevalon led into a series of deep-cut roadless canyons, as work crews from the company would soon discover. This country was unlike any the Pennsylvania men had ever seen—even at other Arizona job sites.

The camp had one redeeming feature: it was brand new and designed for year-round occupation. The buildings were all of frame construction; there were no tents. Officially the buildings were classed as portable, and indeed they were, but building crews had learned a lot about solid construction since the early days of the CCC. They knew how to build a wooden structure that would hold heat. The camp buildings were as modern as anything the CCC had previously used. After almost two years of continuous occupation, the camp was still a model of how things should be done. "The buildings were in very good condition," and inspectors rated the place as "superior type, spotlessly clean, well equipped and furnished."[1]

The camp was new and the scenery beautiful, but there was one disturbing element about the new environment. None of their previous camp assignments had prepared the Pennsylvania boys for the isolation of Chevalon Canyon. The other camps where the company had served were reasonably close to towns. Not here. Thirty-five miles of dirt road separated Chevalon from Winslow. The isolation contributed to the malady called homesickness.

Homesickness was nothing new. It struck all the CCC camps every day. Even the official records mention it. It was the hidden reason behind many enrollee discharges at camps all across the forest. The situation was no different at Chevalon. Special requests for discharges at Chevalon prompted an investigation by the CCC Director's Office. The investigator's conclusion that the men "were extremely homesick and unable to adjust themselves to the camp" could not have been a surprise. Three months earlier the same inspector had talked to sixty-three enrollees at Chevalon who had become eligible to leave the CCC honorably. He reported that when he asked some of them if they had work waiting for them at home, "most of them replied, 'No.' [They] like the camp but cannot get used to the isolation."[2]

Charlie Pflugh was on his way west to catch up with Company 3346. He didn't think much about homesickness on the train ride out to his new assignment in Arizona. He did find himself alone, but he figured on teaming up with other Pennsylvania boys when he arrived at the camp, so everything would be fine. He figured wrong:

> The train trip was somewhat uneventful but I did talk to a number of boys who were going west for CCC duty. They must have been going to other camps because I don't recall any of them getting off the train with me at Winslow. When I got off there was a truck waiting to take me to Camp F-78-A at Chevalon Canyon.

The ride through the high open desert country and into the forest was filled with anticipation. How far was it? What would the camp look like? Would he get along with the other enrollees? As the dirt road narrowed and the forest country closed in, a sudden feeling of isolation hit him:

> I had no idea where the camp was or where I was going. I didn't know anybody at camp either. Those fellows were Pennsylvania men like me but they were from the eastern part of the state, around Philadelphia. (Pflugh interview, 16 November 1999)

Chevalon had been operating for about ten months before Charlie got there, and the work routine was pretty well set. He looked for someone to give him good advice about getting the proper work assignment, but it took awhile before he could get the work that was truly best for him. In the meantime, he had to get used to hard duty. Shortly after arriving he found himself on the Chevalon Canyon road-building crew. It was hard work, Charlie recalled:

> Camp F-78-A work was divided up among several foremen who were in charge of different projects. For example, Francis Bealey was in charge of all forestry work such as pruning, axing, clearing brush, etc. He also had a big share of the firefighting crews when needed. Francis also was in charge of fence building. I worked on installing drainage ditches along the major road into camp. I also worked behind a rock crusher on this road, as well as using a hydraulic air drill to break up big rocks. This was a

tough job. The Chevalon Canyon road was very windy and dangerous because there were no guard rails. If you went off, they just sent your body home in a box. (Pflugh letter, 2 October 1999)

Things were tough at first, but Charlie was not one to complain. Ultimately he would find himself working at less strenuous jobs. He got an assignment as the camp's assistant supply steward, but Charlie most enjoyed working with the education adviser, Manuel Puente. Charlie helped with tutoring and other details of the camp's education program, and Mr. Puente instructed his young assistant on darkroom photography and audiovisual equipment operation. Charlie also was a staff contributor to the camp newspaper. All in all, he was very satisfied with life at Chevalon:

> I don't recall any real hardships at camp. There were a few work injuries to hands, fingers, and legs, but serious harm did not occur very often. You must remember that a lot of these kids were "green" as hell and accidents would happen. We had an ambulance at camp and a physician named H. E. Pinkerton. Some of our CCC boys helped staff the "hospital" room where I spent some time recovering from pneumonia. (Pflugh interview, 16 November 1999; letter, 4 November 1999)

Charles Pflugh at the bottom of Chevalon Canyon, August 1940, three months into his tour of duty. Courtesy Charles Pflugh.

Charlie worked on projects large and small after his recovery. He was assigned to a side camp at Clay Springs with fifteen to twenty other enrollees—the same area where Marshall Wood had worked on prairie dog extermination in 1933–34. This time, Charlie and his crew were clearing a right-of-way and removing dead trees as part of a fire prevention project. Once he recovered from his medical setback, the work helped him become physically fit and mature. He also gained some building skills:

> Another job I remember was construction of a fence on the fringes of the northern desert near the forest [on the north boundary fence line between the national forest and the high open desert of the Colorado Plateau]. We had to dig holes with shovel and picks, cut down some small trees and clear brush before installing the fence wire.
>
> Another major project for F-78-A while I was there was the building of a steel bridge over Chevalon Canyon. It was about 85 percent done when I arrived, and was finished in mid-1940. I am not really sure if it is still used. (Pflugh letter, 4 November 1999)

The crossing is still in use, but the steel bridge the CCC built has been replaced with a one-lane concrete span.

Work was the reason the men were in the woods, but like many of the other CCC boys, Charlie remembered the good times at camp more vividly. He had many opportunities during off-hours to walk outside the camp, enjoy the fresh air, and investigate the wild country around him. The men enjoyed sharing stories of wildlife encounters, and Charlie had a good one:

> The most outrageous incident involving wildlife happened when a bunch of us were on our way back to camp from a day's work. Our foreman, Francis Bealey, spotted a large badger that had run across the road. He told the driver to stop and then called us to follow him and capture the critter. Only a few of us had ever heard of or seen a creature like this before. We soon found out what it could do. We got our pruning saws and ran to catch up to the badger. With great effort, we trapped the animal and forced it into a burlap sack. We then brought it back to the truck and put the sack in the back with ten or twelve of the CCC boys.
>
> We started back to camp and were only a few yards away when this mean old critter decided he had had enough. He

ripped open a big hole in the bag and jumped out into the back of the truck where we were all seated. He looked mean as the devil. We yelled to the driver to stop *now.* I don't remember if we were fully stopped, but the ten guys and myself jumped the high rails of the truck and didn't care. We just wanted to get away from that badger. Francis told us to go after him. We were foolish enough to try but couldn't get him into another bag.

That very same evening, we received the final "punch line." We happened to be showing a movie about wild animals in our area. The show carried an episode about badgers. The main message involved a big warning about how ferocious badgers could be when cornered. After viewing this film, no one, I mean no one, had any desire to go back for a second try at that animal. (Pflugh letter, 2 October 1999)

Chevalon Canyon was one of the few all-weather CCC camps in Arizona. That was convenient because the men didn't need to pack up and move to a desert camp during the winter months. However, winter at a cold-weather camp had its own set of problems. Working outdoors in cold conditions was difficult enough, but conditions inside the camp were perhaps even more challenging. Confinement indoors exacerbated personal disagreements among the men, but more important, it increased the sense of isolation that was always lurking in the back of each enrollee's mind. The officials at Chevalon knew that too, and they tried to help in small ways. The camp newspaper reported, "Since this camp anticipates a considerable amount of inclement weather this winter, the company commander has seen fit to request 2 movies per week to be shown on Friday and Sunday nights."[3] Charlie Pflugh vividly recalled those long winter days:

Things were sometimes tough during the winter. We all tried to find something to do. Men stayed in the barracks playing cards, writing letters, or going over to the Canteen to buy candy or the Education Building to read a book or watch a movie. Card games were strictly reserved for the barracks because it was less conspicuous. I think the camp officers looked the other way when it came to gambling and playing cards for money. There just wasn't that much to do.

We had a camp barber nicknamed "Black Jack" who was also a card shark, and he made some of the boys poor right after pay day. I'm glad that I wasn't hooked on cards, but for those who participated, they had a good time no matter what. There wasn't much money around anyway. It is very difficult to realize today the fun we had with such little money. We only could keep five dollars a month. The rest we sent home, although when you reached a higher ranking in the CCC you could keep eight dollars spending money for the month instead of the usual five. That was a big deal. (Pflugh letter, 2 October 1999)

Another big deal was meals. Feeding two hundred young men each day was a task unto itself. But that was the army's problem. The boys enjoyed the abundance, taste, and variety. Charlie's remembrances are probably typical of most camps:

Our camp food at the regular meal times was just super. The portions were large and it was all you could eat. Several of the boys including myself actually gained weight in the CCCs, even after doing all that work. We were often away from camp at lunch time, and the foreman or Forest Service supervisor would bring out sandwiches and drinks for our noon meal. (Pflugh letter, 2 October 1999)

The cooks at almost every CCC camp put extra effort into preparing holiday meals. Special menus were printed on festive colored paper,

Fresh snowfall at Chevalon Canyon camp F-78-A, one of only two camps occupied during the winter months in the Rim Country, 1940–41. Courtesy Charles Pflugh.

complete with a drawing or cartoon by the camp artist. Choices of main dishes and desserts were expanded and made appropriate to the celebration. There was pumpkin pie for Thanksgiving, cherry pie on George Washington's birthday, and ice cream sundaes for the Fourth of July. Camp records from Chevalon Canyon camp show that cooks pulled out all the stops to make dining special at holiday time. Charlie took notice:

> What I really remember were the holiday meals. Even though they were served at camp, we went all out. Special menus were printed and all of the traditional food items were served. On Thanksgiving Day, 1940, we had roast turkey with dressing and mashed potatoes, plus other items too numerous to mention. There was pumpkin pie and ice cream for dessert. It was wonderful. (Pflugh interview, 16 November 1999)

Charlie's CCC experience was coming to an end just as world war was closing in on America. In April 1941 his company was transferred to Columbia Falls, Montana:

> Our CCC group never came back to Arizona. It looked like there was going to be war, so CCC work slacked off a bit. I was discharged in June 1941. I will never forget my time at F-78-A in Arizona. I can truly say that the CCC was the best time in my life. Without hesitation, the CCC turned this country around and built its superstructure back to "Grade A." For the men, it meant life or death to thousands, in fact millions, of men who were just existing at the time, rather than fully living.

Since then, I have enjoyed my very happy home life, but I still can say that the CCC's were the best times of my life. (Pflugh letter, 4 November 1999)[4]

Chapter 9

The Final Years: Richard Thim

Growing up in Chandler, Arizona, Richard Thim was no stranger to outdoor work:

> I got a job weeding cotton fields for ten cents a row, and they were long rows. I would work all day and maybe get a dollar fifty. My dad had some difficult times too. He worked at whatever job he could get. Times were tough trying to support a family. One day he saw a story in the paper about the CCC and we talked about it. I was in my second year of high school, but I decided to quit and join up. I ended up first going to Phoenix to get a physical exam. I had felt a little lonely that first day until I heard someone say, "Hello, Richard." I looked up, and there was a friend of mine from the days when I was weeding cotton. We stuck together after that and I didn't feel so bad. After that, they boarded us on trains and we made our way to Holbrook. We really had no special training at CCC-type work beforehand.

No special fanfare greeted Richard when his group arrived at Blue Camp. "They simply met us with trucks," he remembered, "and drove us south toward the forest" (Thim interview, 30 October 1999).

There were formal rules to be learned when new enrollees arrived at camp. Orientation started with special instructions on camp behavior and etiquette delivered by the supervising army officer, either via direct contact or in the camp newspaper. Richard said that most of the rules were "by the [military] book" and mirrored army barracks regulations. The new arrivals got a less formal education when they had the opportunity to mingle with their bunkmates. Most of the advice was common sense. Experienced enrollees gently tried to remind the new fellows that proper behavior was expected. One camp newspaper suggested that the men treat their tents as they would their homes:

> Don't throw your cigarettes or matches on the floor . . . do not talk after the lights are out, and treat your tent mates as you would your brothers. . . . [T]here is enough water to take baths and wash your hands and face as often as they need it.

Those using the recreation building were told:

> There is no profanity allowed and you are the one to see that it is not used. If you miss a shot while playing pool, think before you curse, or someone has to politely ask you to leave.

Old-timers would sometimes take problem recruits aside and "talk" to them about their conduct.[1]

In camp, the men had two sets of clothes. In the early days there was no standard uniform for everyday work; blue denim pants and any old work shirt were good enough. Enrollees were given a dress uniform that included a shirt, tie, and trousers, all of which had a wartime look. Many young men correctly suspected they were World War I surplus. Richard didn't particularly like his uniform no matter where it came from. It was made of scratchy wool, and the pants were uncomfortably narrow at the ankles. On a visit to an eastern camp in 1938, President Franklin Roosevelt didn't like the look either. He ordered new spruce green uniforms to be given to all enrollees, although they didn't make it into general circulation until the following year.[2] Later in the program, green and yellow CCC insignia patches for coats and hats were also issued.

Richard's immediate problem at Blue camp was to get rid of the rough wool clothing, but it was October 1940 and cold temperatures were just around the corner. One thing he certainly wanted to hang on to was a dependable winter coat:

> I remember they issued us a Mackinaw coat that was similar to a peacoat that the Navy used. It was heavy and warm. It wasn't a month before it got stolen. I went to the army commander and reported it. He said, "When we line the men up for inspection, you go down the row and pick out your coat." Well, how am I going to pick out my coat from all of the others that the guys are wearing? So I said no. Instead I made the announcement in the barracks that I knew who took it and there would be no trouble if the coat was left on my bed when I came back from supper. Of

course I didn't know who took it, but the bluff must have worked because sure enough, I found the coat lying on my bed when I came back. (Thim interview, 30 October 1999)

Richard quickly noticed that many of the enrollees at Blue camp were not from Arizona. He also noticed that living in the forest affected those newcomers differently:

After I had been there for a while, we got some new boys from Texas. They must have been homesick because after the first month about fifteen or twenty of them "went over the hill" and started walking for home. Down at the Blue Camp you are sur-rounded by mountains and you don't really see out. Those boys from Texas were used to the wide-open plains, and I suppose just couldn't take it there on the Blue. (Thim interview, 30 October 1999)

Richard served two enlistment periods in the CCC, but he wasn't there long before he figured out that some job assignments were better than others:

Guys felt fortunate to be a truck driver. All they had to do was take you out to the job and drive you back again. Some crews used jackhammers to break up rock and lay it down on the Red Hill Road. I'm glad I didn't get on that job. I didn't mind fence building too much. I did that kind of work before, when I was in Chandler, so I was pretty well skilled. On one of our CCC jobs we went east on the road to Pueblo Park and built the state boundary fence between Arizona and New Mexico. (Thim interview, 30 October 1999)

Like many enrollees, Richard discovered that the truly memorable events of CCC life did not take place on the job site, or even on leave or vacation:

Back at camp we had a guy named Bill Brimhall of Mesa, Arizona. It was decided that the camp needed a night watchman, someone to keep the buildings heated during the night and generally care for things, and Bill got the job. He got to sleep during the day when the rest of us were working, but he had to be up at night watching over the place. One night he had made a snack for himself and was taking the leftovers out to the garbage when he spotted a large black dog a short distance away. When he approached, he noticed instead that it was a bear. He turned and made a mad dash for the door. He was so scared that he smashed directly into the screen door. It was like he was trying to run right through the screen to get to the safety of the barracks. After that incident, I don't think he wanted to be the night watchman anymore. (Thim interview, 30 October 1999)

The official records of the Mogollon Rim and White Mountain CCC camps contain little evidence of racial tensions or conflicts, but it seems safe to assume that some incidents did occur. Perhaps they were unknown to authorities and were worked out at the moment of disagreement. Richard talked about an incident that authorities knew about, although it never found its way into the official record:

The Hispanics from Texas had their own barracks with a common wash area in between the buildings at Blue camp. One of our guys had been drinking some extract or something else to make himself feel good, and he got the idea that he was going to fight the "Mexicans." He got a butcher knife and went over to the wash area. One of them saw him coming and hit him in the side of the head with an empty metal bucket. The fellow came back to our barracks and showed us what the kid had done. He talked a bunch of the guys into going to the tool shed and getting picks and going over to their barracks to even the score. It wasn't the fault of the Texans, but it was made to sound that way. The camp commander finally came out and settled things down. They also hosed down the fellow who started it, and that seemed to end the whole thing. (Thim interview, 30 October 1999)

Richard had an advantage when it came to going home once in awhile on leave. His hometown of Chandler, Arizona, wasn't exactly close to the camp on the Blue, but it was sure a lot closer than Texas. Richard knew that the camp commanders were more likely to make arrangements for local boys to go home occasionally, but that didn't seem unfair to him. The locals were more likely to come back and were more easily found if they went AWOL. The out-of-state boys might get the idea that the authorities would be less likely to come after them, and in fact that was true. Despite the convenience of being a local boy, Richard still had difficulty getting home on leave:

Getting home now and then with little money could be a problem. At Christmas time we found a fellow who had a big long-bed truck and we paid him to drive about fifteen of us to Phoenix. We came down through the Salt River Canyon, and the road was a lot more narrow back then. With all of us in the back, the truck was so heavy that when we hit a dip in the road the front end of the truck would come up off the pavement. That was spooky.

Another time, I was headed home on leave and a bunch of us made it to Show Low before we ran out of money. At that time there was very little in Show Low, not much more than a service station and café. We spent the last little bit of money we had on coffee and a slice of pie, and got out on the road to hitch a ride. We waited for quite a while before one of the guys said that we would have to split up in order for someone to stop and give us a ride. The first guy got a ride right away, but we had to wait a while longer before an Apache came along and gave us a ride to Globe. We got another ride from there to Mesa. From there I had to walk the three miles home. It turns out that my dad passed me on the road in his car but didn't recognize me. It must have been my larger physical appearance and that heavy coat. In any event, I had to walk the rest of the way home without a ride. (Thim interview, 30 October 1999)

Youthful road crew from Blue camp F-03-A, 1940–41. Richard Thim is at left. Courtesy Richard Thim.

Completion of repairs on the state line fence, 1940–41.
Richard Thim (right) and enrollee Rick Solesbee celebrate
a job well done. Courtesy Richard Thim.

Embarrassing incidents were common around camp. Most of those
episodes have taken on comic overtones and with the passage of time
have become easier to talk about. Richard didn't mind telling this one
on himself:

> In the winter at Blue, we had some free time so I made a snow
> sled. I used metal barrel bands for the skids and it worked pretty
> well. A couple of friends and me walked from camp and started
> up the Pueblo Park Road. Just then a truck came by and we got
> a ride farther up the road to where the sledding was better. We
> even had shovels that we would sit on and hold the handle as we

slid down the road. We had a great time, but when we started back at the end of the day we discovered it was a very long walk back without a ride. After a while I came across a canyon off the road that I thought was Johnson Canyon—the one that would lead right to camp. The others weren't sure, so I started off by myself. The canyon bottom was dense with trees and a little spooky, but it turned out it was the right route and I ended up in camp before them.

When I got in, the rest of the guys were telling me what a great meal I had missed: the best chicken the camp had to offer. I went to the mess hall but it was too late. Back then we hardly ever took a sandwich or anything for lunch, so it had been awhile since my last meal. I finally went out to the garbage cans. I looked in and could see there was almost a full yellow cake sitting right there on top. I was desperate. I looked around to see if anyone was looking before I reached in and got two pieces out of the middle. That was it for the evening, but at least I got something. Later my two friends came in to camp and found absolutely nothing left to eat. (Thim interview, 30 October 1999)

Richard Thim and Gene Gaddy were at the Blue camp together from October 1940 until February 1941, when Gene was honorably discharged. By then, Gene had become the camp's assistant leader—or "top kick," as the enrollees called him. "You don't get that honor handed to you unless you can show them what you can do," Richard recalled (Thim interview, 30 October 1999).

By the time Richard was into his second tour of duty on the Blue, talk of war was more frequent. Late-night conversations in the barracks were about the war in Europe. Was America going to be a part of it? What did their future hold? What would happen to the CCC? By the summer of 1941 men were being drafted right out of the CCC camps; at least two left from Blue. Richard was honorably discharged from the CCC in October 1941, exactly one year after his original CCC enlistment. For a short time afterward he worked on a chicken farm in Chandler, but world events soon overtook him. When the United States entered the war, Richard fulfilled his military duty and saw action in Europe at Normandy and at the Battle of the Bulge in 1944. His wartime memories are a great deal more harrowing than his CCC recollections, but that is another story.[3]

Chapter 10

Farewell to the CCC

At the end of the first enlistment period, an enrollee had two choices: he could sign up for another six-month tour of duty, or he could go home. For those going home, there was no fanfare, no awards dinner, no special ceremony. A few friends might get together and share some memories, but the nature of the CCC program did not fit with ceremonial farewells.

The men who enrolled later in the program had different discharge dates from those of earlier enrollees, of course, and were usually placed in companies to fill vacant slots. These men trickled out of the companies as their enlistments expired. Ranks were also depleted by discharges for health reasons and by desertions. Over several enlistment periods, the entire camp roster could turn over, leaving only enrollees who were not present when the company was originally formed.[1]

The camp newspapers tried to keep up with the comings and goings. Often the paper would include a paragraph congratulating those who were moving on—some of them back home, others to jobs outside the CCC. The names of the few remaining original enrollees still left in camp might be proudly printed in the paper too.

The camp commanders took notice of the turnover and sometimes used the paper to wish them good luck. Ernest Massad of Blue camp wrote this editorial printed on page one of the March 1940 *Blue Buffalo:*

> I know that there are many things including trades and professions that most of you men have learned since you first joined the Civilian Conservation Corps. . . . You are leaving and going into you communities to become part of that community . . . and will take the places of the leading citizens of that commu-

nity. . . . What you have learned in the Civilian Conservation Corps will inevitably make you fit into that community. . . . We will from time to time hear from you or about you, and will point with pride to your success. . . . The best of luck to you and if I can ever be of service to you, just call on me.

The CCC was a hugely popular relief program that would almost certainly have continued in some form had it not been for America's entry into World War II. Yet even before the war there were signs that the program was beginning to weaken. Economic conditions in the country were improving. Applications for the CCC dropped. Desertions from the camps increased as more men gravitated to jobs in the civilian sector. By the summer of 1941 the program counted fewer that 200,000 men in about 900 camps, versus a 1935 level of 500,000 enrollees serving in 2,600 camps. Some who had previously stood behind the CCC now questioned whether the program was necessary in light of the need for a stronger national defense.[2]

When the war finally came to America, Congress nevertheless engaged in a spirited debate over whether to continue funding for the CCC. In the end, after several close votes, Congress admitted the inevitable and ordered the camps closed and their property disposed of. In fact, the camp disposal process had been a part of the CCC plan since the program's early years. Most of the camps on the Rim and in the White Mountains had completed their work and closed long before war came.

In the few camps that were still up and running, change was in the air. The war in Europe had been going on since 1939, and rumors about U.S. involvement were an inevitable part of camp conversations. By 1941, many CCC reenlistments were being disallowed as the peacetime draft in America reached down into the camps to claim enrollees. The camp superintendent at East Verde was put on terminal leave in mid-1941, mostly because so many companies had been disbanded. The army commanders at Blue, Chevalon Canyon, and East Verde camps began offering classes in military drill, officially called "national defense training."

The military lifestyle of the CCC did make for an easier transition into the wartime army. Enrollees were used to discipline and following orders. They were used to uniforms and barracks inspection and army food. At basic training the army leadership sought them out—sometimes with comic results. Richard Thim remembered being asked by the drill instructor if anyone in the ranks had been in the CCC:

Another fellow and I raised our hands, and the sergeant pulled us out of line and put us on KP [kitchen police] duty. I learned then to keep quiet. (Thim interview, 30 October 1999)

Such incidents notwithstanding, most CCC alumni moved easily into military life; many made good noncommissioned officers. Charlie Pflugh's organizational skills and experience as a supply steward at Chevalon Canyon

provided me with a wonderful background when I joined the U.S. Army two years later. I became a supply sergeant in no time, which of course gave me a few extra bucks each month. It also gave me the opportunity to precede my outfit overseas with Captain Joe Smith . . . to set up our large medical unit.

As an added bonus, a military paper snafu gave Charlie additional time to see London at his leisure (Pflugh letter, 2 October 1999).

The Japanese attack on Pearl Harbor on 7 December 1941 effectively spelled the end of the CCC. War mobilization became the first priority. Congress ordered the men discharged by July 1942 (presumably ready for induction into the military), and all camp property disposed of by the end of that year. Men who served out their CCC enlistment were awarded an honorable discharge that included a "Record of Service"

Crescent Lake side camp, November 1934. This crew's assignment was to make improvements on the lake dam. Courtesy Apache-Sitgreaves National Forests.

with their service dates, company and headquarters, the type of work in which they were engaged (carpentry, bridges, etc.), and a general performance rating.

As for the camps, everything, down to the last box of nails, was to be accounted for and sold. The land on which the camps sat would revert to the previous owner—not a complicated process on the national forests since all camps (except for Bar X Ranch, and possibly Eagle Creek) had been set up on Forest Service land. But what happened to the buildings?

Most of the forest camps were already gone by 1941. Hart Canyon, Three Forks, Greer, and Bar X Ranch were mostly tent sites, and the gear had long since been shifted to other camps and other uses, leaving nothing behind. But Chevalon Canyon was only two years old, with frame buildings meant to withstand winters on the Mogollon Plateau. Blue camp, the granddaddy of the Arizona forests, had also been built to survive the mountain winters. The way these two camps were closed is a good example of how things were handled for all the remaining camps at the end of the CCC program.

The instructions from Congress were clear: everything had to go— but where? The army had anticipated moving the buildings as CCC work moved from place to place, and the semipermanent construction meant that tear-down was not a big problem. In the final months, bids were submitted from various sources, but with a war on, government agencies were always first in line. The buildings at Blue were transferred to the Federal Public Housing Administration in San Francisco. The land itself was still too useful to ignore, so later the Blue Elementary School was built over what was once the recreation and mess hall. The buildings at Chevalon Canyon were transferred to the War Department and moved to Luke Air Base west of Phoenix. Like most of the CCC men, the buildings went to war, too. In this case, they became troop housing on the base.[3]

The boys and men of the CCC left a lasting legacy for Arizona. A drive over just about any of the forest roads off the main highway will take you to some old CCC job site. Roads, campgrounds, buildings, and occasional ruins all have the mark of the CCC on them. The stone flag base at Indian Gardens east of Payson is still there, including the plaque left by the first group of enrollees to serve at the camp. The stone-pillared camp shelters at Juan Miller campground north of Clifton on the Coronado Trail stand exactly as they did when the CCC boys put them up

Mess call at Hart Canyon camp F-21-A, August 1933. The following year the camp was closed; the tents were taken down for use at other sites. Courtesy Apache-Sitgreaves National Forests.

in the 1930s. That site is the most intact and complete evidence of CCC campground construction left in the forests of northeastern Arizona.[4]

The remaining veterans of CCC service have found that revisiting the past can be a bittersweet experience. In 1940 Bill Dean served at Flagstaff, Camp F-80-A. In 1983 he made a sentimental journey from his home in Pennsylvania to his former duty station out West:

> My old F-80-A site is now—what else—a housing development. But after I was out of town and able to get around I was happy to see a sight I could hardly believe. The hundreds of 8–10-inch quaking aspen I had planted along the road to the Grand Canyon so long ago were now 35–40-foot beautiful tall trees. That alone was worth the trip. (Dean letter, 20 April 2001)

In 1935 Al Purdy worked for the Forest Service at remote Buffalo Crossing in the White Mountains. His wife, Betty, lived nearby. She hated to leave when his job was finally done, and they returned to the area many times:

> For many years, my family has gone back to that area for the best camping, fishing, and scenery. I went through there in May [2001] and found a few changes, but the scenery is as wonderful as ever.[5]

In many places where the CCC operated there is nothing but beautiful scenery to look at today. But imagination is a powerful force in the woods. A short walk away from the flagpole monument at Indian Gardens near Kohl's Ranch, it becomes easy to visualize rows of tents and the hurried activity of crews loading tools onto trucks and preparing for another day of roadwork. What did those CCC boys from Texas think about before they went to sleep on that first cold night at Los Burros camp near the tiny town of Pinetop? What about the boys from Pennsylvania who came to Chevalon camp? When they walked to the edge of the canyon and looked up at the clear night sky, did they have the same middle-of-nowhere feeling that modern-day campers often experience when they set up camp miles from the main highway? At Buffalo Crossing, modern campers don't even have to leave the campground to think about what it would be like to spend a summer there. They just need to know that a CCC camp was right underneath their feet. The CCC boys slept there in tents too and experienced the same frightening nighttime thunderstorms with lightning that shatters nearby pine trees.

We will never know everything the CCC boys did, but the usefulness of their projects is still clear even if some of their actual work can no longer be seen. Over the years, crews from the U.S. Forest Service have updated old CCC jobs. Campgrounds the CCC first built, like Winn, Chevalon Crossing, and Tonto Creek, have been remodeled. Boundary fencing put up in the 1930s on the northern sections of the Sitgreaves Forest has been replaced. Check dams on the river near Greer have been improved. The bridges across the Blue River were redone in the 1950s. The bungalow-style Alpine Ranger Station has been replaced by a more functional but less charming facility. All of these and more began as CCC projects.

The original work may be hard to find, but the actual construction was never the most important thing about the CCC. Most important then and now are the men themselves—Roosevelt's "Tree Army." They completed countless projects and learned lasting lessons for themselves in the process. Charlie Pflugh eloquently summarized the value of the experience for himself:

> Those who spent time in the CCC did so much to build their bodies up physically. Some of the most important things we learned were cleanliness, obedience, and how to live with each other. These qualities play a major role in life and gave the CCC

boys a jump-start in World War II. (Pflugh interview, 30 September 1999)

The enrollees who worked on the Mogollon Rim and White Mountains can be found all across America today. But their numbers are decreasing. Family members know of their adventures in the woods, but few others do. CCC survivors have formed national and local alumni associations to keep the memories alive. They too will fade, of course, but the CCC nevertheless left behind a lasting record of accomplishments, and for that the young men who were a part of it deserve the gratitude of the nation.

The boys called it "the best years of my life." The CCC program was spectacularly successful as a character builder for young men, as an educational outreach program for them during troubled times, and as a huge step forward in forest health and management. National leaders as well as small-town citizens living near the camps knew this in the 1930s. The challenge for Americans in the future is to keep the lessons, adventures, and accomplishments of that era alive after the CCC boys leave us.

CCC Forest Camps in the Mogollon Rim/White Mountains of Arizona, 1933–42

Camp #	Camp Name	Post Office	Date Established
F-03-A	Blue	Blue	11 June 1933
F-04-A	——	Springerville	27 May 1933
F-21-A	Hart Canyon	Winslow	29 May 1933
F-22-A	Los Burros	McNary	5 June 1933
F-23-A	Indian Gardens	Payson	24 May 1933
F-24-A	Bar X Ranch	Young	13 June 1933
F-48-A	Eagle Creek	Clifton	20 August 1935
F-54-A	Buffalo Crossing	Springerville	5 May 1934
F-55-A	Three Forks	Alpine	10 May 1934
F-65-A	Juan Miller	Clifton	fall 1935
F-75-A	Pivot Rock	Flagstaff	29 May 1937
F-76-A	Greer	Springerville	28 May 1938
F-77-A	East Verde	Pine	6 September 1939
F-78-A	Chevalon Canyon	Winslow	27 June 1939

FIRE LOOKOUTS IN THE RIM COUNTRY

Perhaps as important as firefighting in the CCC was the place-ment and building of fire lookout towers. In its early days, the Forest Service, short of both manpower and money, used very primitive methods of finding fires. The most common way to scout fires was by using "lag" trees. Foresters picked out a tall, strong pine and spiked it with metal bolts, then used the tree as a type of ladder. Occasionally a small platform was built at the top. The metal steps did not kill the tree, but the climb was dan-gerous and seldom gave an observer a good above-the-treetops view. After finding the smoke, the ranger was expected to climb down, pick up tools, and head for the fire.[1]

The next logical step was towers with viewing platforms. Many were built before the CCC arrived, but the added manpower made it possible to accelerate new construction and to repair and enlarge existing towers (see table 1). Such construction often included a storage building and small living quarters at the base of the tower.

During the CCC days, the Forest Service used a standardized plan for lookout construction. The Aermotor Company of Chi-cago manufactured prefabricated parts for steel towers and had been sending them out to the forests since the 1920s. With the new manpower from the CCC and the relative ease of building using prefab units, lookout tower construction jumped ahead in all the country's forest regions.[2]

Because the Mogollon Rim escarpment stretches across half the state, the views are perfect for fire observation. From the edge one can look down on the central basins and also turn to see across the level plateau to the north. The canyons that cut the Rim on top and flow to the north get progressively steeper and more difficult to cross, even by road. Yet the canyon heads do not extend to the edge of the Rim. The area closest to the edge is flat. It would not have been difficult for CCC crews to get build-ing materials and manpower to the lookout sites on the Rim. Thus, Forest Service officials planned for a string of towers along the Mogollon Rim and on selected mountaintop sites farther east in the Apache National Forest.

Even though it was geologically easier to build on the edge of the Rim, the earliest towers were built on the high mountain sites in eastern Arizona. Indeed, within two months of opening one of the first Arizona camps, F-04-A near Alpine, a CCC crew of twenty was starting work on the Escudilla tower atop the third highest mountain in the state. That same camp also had a crew of fifteen men working on a tower near KP Cienega on the Coronado Trail south of Hannagan Meadow.

On the Tonto National Forest, Diamond Point juts out below the rim, providing an ideal view of the Payson-to-Young territory—some of the most rugged in central Arizona. The CCC built a thirty-foot-tall standard tower here in the fall of 1936. While modifications have since been made to the tower, the wood-frame cabin at the base built in 1941 is little changed. The tower itself can easily be seen by motorists looking north of State Route 260 a short distance from Payson.

Besides new towers, the CCC also rebuilt or made modifications to existing fire towers. When Promontory tower on the Sitgreaves forest was built in 1924, it was the tallest lookout in the country—110 feet. In 1938 the CCC boys replaced the original ladder with steel stairs crisscrossing inside the tower frame, making the climb less nerve-racking.[3]

Table 1. Fire Lookout Towers Built by the CCC in the Mogollon Rim/White Mountains Region

Lookout	Date	National Forest
Bear Mountain	1933	Apache-Sitgreaves
Big Lake	1933	Apache-Sitgreaves
Blue	1933	Apache-Sitgreaves
Escudilla	1933	Apache-Sitgreaves
P. S. Knoll	1933	Apache-Sitgreaves
Springer Mountain	1933	Apache-Sitgreaves
Dutch Joe	1940	Apache-Sitgreaves
Baker Butte	1937	Coconino
Diamond Point	1936	Tonto

From USDA Forest Service, *Cultural Resource Management, Lookouts in the Southwestern Region.* Report 8. September 1989.

Diamond Point lookout tower, Tonto National Forest, September 1937. Courtesy Northern Gila County Historical Society, Inc.

The original tower at Baker Butte on the Coconino National Forest was built in 1922. The butte itself is the highest point on the Mogollon Rim, and it offers spectacular views south toward Payson and the Mazatzal wilderness beyond. In 1937 the CCC boys took down the wooden structure and replaced it with the standard MC-24 steel tower—the tower design preferred for the southwestern forests.

INTRODUCTION: RELIEF FROM HARD TIMES

1. *NACCCA Journal* (St. Louis, Mo.) 21, no. 3 (March 1998): 4. Assistant leaders were paid $36 per month. Five staff personnel—mess, supply, top sergeant, etc.—earned $45 per month. Harry Dallas, the executive director of the NACCCA, noted that Congress adjusted the enrollee pay scale several times over the life of the program. Over the life of the CCC program in Arizona, enrollees sent home a total of $3.7 million as part of their monthly wages. See Ray Hoyt, *"We Can Take It": A Short Story of the C.C.C.* (New York: American Book Company, 1935), 23, for details on enlistment and discharge requirements.

2. John A. Salmond, *The Civilian Conservation Corps, 1933–1942: A New Deal Case Study* (Durham: Duke University Press, 1967), 116.

3. Alison T. Otis, William D. Honey, Thomas C. Hogg, and Kimberly K. Lakin, *The Forest Service and the Civilian Conservation Corps: 1933–42* (Washington, D.C.: U.S. Department of Agriculture, Forest Service, FS-395, 1986), 8.

4. Only in rare cases was more than one company assigned to a single camp. The company number was based on the nine army corps areas in the United States. Arizona, New Mexico, and Texas were in the 8th Army Corps. Men recruited from those states were thus organized into companies beginning with the number 8. Company 842, for example, was formed in the Southwest. In the late 1930s several companies of Pennsylvania men from the 3rd Army Corps, organized in the East, were sent to Arizona; their units can be easily identified as well—Company 3346, for instance. In some cases the second number in the company ID was the corps number. See *NACCCA Journal* 21, no. 12 (December 1998): 6.

5. Charles W. Pflugh, telephone interviews with the author, 30 September 1999, 28 October 1999, and 16 November 1999; letter of 2 October 1999. Subsequent references to these sources and to a letter to the author of 4 November 1999 will appear parenthetically in the text.

CHAPTER 1: THE CCC IN ARIZONA

1. Grand Canyon National Park visitors who make their way to the Yavapai Observation Station on the South Rim can see a small display of CCC memorabilia and pick up a pamphlet, *The Civilian Conservation Corps at Grand Canyon Village,* which serves as a self-guided tour of CCC sites in the area. For a history of a CCC unit working

at the Grand Canyon, see Louis Purvis, *The Ace in the Hole: A Brief History of Company 818 of the Civilian Conservation Corps* (Columbus, Ga.: Brentwood Christian Press, 1989). See also Peter Booth, "The Civilian Conservation Corps in Arizona, 1933–1942" (master's thesis, University of Arizona, 1991).

2. Robert D. Baker, Robert S. Maxwell, Victor H. Treat, and Henry C. Dethloff, *Timeless Heritage: A History of the Forest Service in the Southwest* (Washington, D.C.: U.S. Department of Agriculture, Forest Service, FS-409, 1988), 54.

3. This policy is also consistent with the policy of generally keeping workers within the same army corps area, in this case the 8th Corps. See William S. Collins, *The New Deal in Arizona* (Phoenix: Arizona State Parks Board, 1999), 209.

4. In later years, the Soil Conservation Service (SCS) would work on private land. See Peter Booth, "Cactizonians: The Civilian Conservation Corps in Pima County, 1933–1942," *Journal of Arizona History* 32 (autumn 1991): 313.

5. Gregory R. Seymour, *The Civilian Conservation Corps in Southeast Arizona: An Overview of Fifteen Soil Conservation and Department of Grazing Camps in Graham and Greenlee Counties, Southeast Arizona* (SWCA Archaeological Report No. 95-13, 13 January 1995, prepared for Bureau of Land Management, Safford District, Ariz.), 9. See also Booth, "The CCC in Arizona," 130.

6. Halbert A. Burch, "CCC History Underway," *Arizona Historical Society Magazine* 4, no. 6 (1987): 3. A jobs and money outline of benefits to Arizona can also be found in John Irish's file at Coconino National Forest, Flagstaff, Ariz. The document is a photocopy from the National Archives, Record Group 35, entry 67, entitled "Federal Security Agency, Civilian Conservation Corps: A Brief Summary of Certain Phases of the CCC Program—Arizona. Period April 1933–June 30, 1942."

7. Tom Brokaw's best-selling book *The Greatest Generation* fails to mention the CCC and its contributions.

8. William Dean, letter to the author, 20 April 2001. Subsequent references to this letter will appear parenthetically in the text.

9. Richard Thim, interview with the author, Phoenix, Ariz., 30 October 1999. See also Booth, "Cactizonians"; Camp Inspection Reports, F-22-A, 20 July 1936, 3, National Archives Branch Depository, College Park, Md., Records of the CCC, Record Group 35.

10. Collins, *The New Deal in Arizona,* ch. 9, "The Indian New Deal," 237–72.

11. Ibid., 241–43.

12. Booth, "Cactizonians," 306–07.

13. John Welch, Bureau of Indian Affairs archaeologist, White Mountain

Apache Indian Reservation, telephone conversations with the author, 18 August 1999 and 8 June 2004. See also Baker et al., *Timeless Heritage,* 54; Eugene Morris, National Archives specialist, telephone interview with the author, 8 June 2004. For an overview of the CCC and Native Americans in Arizona, see Collins, *The New Deal in Arizona,* "The Indian New Deal"; and Booth, "The CCC in Arizona."

14. Official records, camp newspapers, and enrollee letters of the time all spell both the area and the camp "Chevalon." Sometime after World War II and continuing into the present (and for reasons unknown to Forest Service officials), maps and official U.S. Forest Service documents began using the spelling "Chevelon." I use "Chevalon" throughout as a way to be true to those reports originating in the 1930s and also to avoid confusing the reader.

15. Otis et al., *The Forest Service and the CCC,* 8–10, 72.

16. "CCC Educational Programs Discussed at Local Meetings," *Arizona Daily Star,* 24 November 1934, from file at Arizona State Capitol Museum Archives, Phoenix.

17. *Noon Creek Echo,* January 1940, Center for Research Libraries, Chicago.

18. Camp Inspection Reports, F-75-A, 13 June 1940, National Archives Branch Depository, College Park, Md., Records of the CCC, Record Group 35.

19. See appendix 2 for a discussion of fire lookout towers.

20. At one point during the 1930s there were forty-five administrative complexes containing about 188 structures on Arizona's national forests. A number of these Depression-era administrative buildings are still standing, and some of them are being put to new uses as the twenty-first century begins. A few selected structures built or updated by the CCC have become available to the public on a rental basis. See Sam Lowe, "Rustic Respites," *Arizona Republic,* 6 September 1999, D1.

21. There were at least two popular bungalow styles to choose from. Whether intended or not, the Forest Service appeared to favor the arts and crafts style (sometimes called the craftsman style) popularized by the brothers Charles and Henry Greene and found in many southern California home designs. Bungalows were usually one story, featured an open floor plan inside, and always included a porch, usually with a low-pitched roof and overhang. The arts and crafts design made extensive use of timber and stone for construction materials (as opposed to the brick and stucco of the Midwest prairie model). Such a design choice appears to be a good fit with the forest environment, and perhaps that is why the Forest Service chose it. For more information, see "America's Homestyles—The Bungalow Special," broadcast by HGTV on 25 September 1999. The Forest Service selected the bungalow style in the 1920s at the height of its popularity, but by the time construction

of the buildings began in the 1930s the style had begun to lose its popularity. Information on existing USFS structures built by the CCC on the Apache-Sitgreaves National Forests provided by USFS staff archaeologists Heather Cooper and Linda Martin. See also U.S. Department of the Interior, National Park Service, National Register of Historic Places, Multiple Property Documentation Form, "Depression Era USDA Forest Service Administrative Complexes in Arizona," E-6, filed with USDA Forest Service, Southwestern Region, Albuquerque, N.M.

22. Betty Purdy Fischer, "Love Affair with State Grew Fast," *Arizona Republic,* 6 January 2002, B9; also Betty Purdy Fischer, telephone interview with author, 20 February 2002.

23. Baker et al., *Timeless Heritage,* 129.

24. Camp Inspection Reports, F-48-A, 23 October 1937, National Archives Branch Depository, College Park, Md., Records of the CCC, Record Group 35.

25. Seymour, *The Civilian Conservation Corps in Southeast Arizona,* 15.

26. Bud Clark, interview with the author, Young, Ariz., 24 March 2001. Bud Clark's father, Elvis, operated the canteen at Bar X Ranch CCC camp. See also Raymond Cline, telephone interview with the author, 13 January 2001.

27. Baker et al., *Timeless Heritage,* 54.

28. Dr. Gene Flanagan, "My Family and the CCC's in Arizona, 1933–41," Flanagan Papers, National Association of CCC Alumni Museum, St. Louis.

29. Kitty Martin Butler (daughter of Fred Martin), interviews with the author, Payson, Ariz., 20 January 2002 and 11 June 2004.

30. Marshall Wood, undated letter to the author, received 26 October 1999. Subsequent references to this letter will appear parenthetically in the text. Also Camp Inspection Reports, F-54-A, 22 May 1940, National Archives Branch Depository, College Park, Md., Records of the CCC, Record Group 35.

31. Camp Inspection Reports, F-75-A, 13 June 1940, 25 June 1941, National Archives Branch Depository, College Park, Md., Records of the CCC, Record Group 35.

32. Camp Inspection Reports, F-54-A, 27 May 1940, National Archives Branch Depository, College Park, Md., Records of the CCC, Record Group 35.

CHAPTER 2: A HISTORY OF THE CCC CAMPS IN ARIZONA'S RIM COUNTRY

1. Seymour, *The Civilian Conservation Corps in Southeast Arizona,* 8; see also *The Civilian Conservation Corps: Coronado National Forest, 1933–1942* (USDA Forest Service, Southwestern Region, 1991) regarding water difficulties in southern Arizona, a list of camps on the forest, and the winter/summer camp switches that were sometimes necessary.

2. Camp Inspection Reports, F-03-A, 20 January 1934, 1 July 1941, National Archives Branch Depository, College Park, Md., Records of the CCC, Record Group 35.

3. *Blue Buffalo*, 5 December 1935 and 6 April 1939, Center for Research Libraries, Chicago.

4. The Marion Watson incident is taken from notes from a videotape taken by Marion Watson in summer 1990. It is part of an interview transcript taken by Kay Read on 21 August 1990 and can be found in the historical file at Alpine Ranger Station, Apache-Sitgreaves National Forests, Alpine, Ariz.

5. Camp Inspection Reports, F-03-A, 16 February 1935, National Archives Branch Depository, College Park, Md., Records of the CCC, Record Group 35.

6. Lt. Col. Elmer E. Huber (ret.), telephone interview with the author, 21 October 1999.

7. A photo in the Alpine Ranger Station shows a company from F-04-A finishing construction on the Stone Creek Road (FR 275) on 4 November 1933. The men are posed with a sign that says Camp Lawton. That may be as close as anyone can get to a name for that camp. However, there is no mention of a Camp Lawton in any official Forest Service record.

8. Those who favor the Jackson Springs site note the dependable water supply there—one that still exists today. Yet the site's terrain seems unsuitable for a camp for two hundred men. There is not enough level ground near the spring for buildings or tents. The area now shows heavy camping and other recreational uses. Off-road vehicle tracks have obliterated any traces or relics of a CCC camp. Another possibility is that this location was a side camp. Side camp records are almost nonexistent, though, so proving that would be almost impossible. Side camps rarely existed for more than a month or so, and almost all were of tent construction without concrete footers or foundations for more permanent structures. The side camp theory is weak because records found in Otis et al., *The Forest Service and the CCC, 1933–42*, 30, for July 1933 show side camps from F-04-A, and none of these is identified as Jackson Springs.

9. Otis et al., *The Forest Service and the CCC, 1933–42*, 30.

10. The photo is displayed in the lobby of the Alpine Ranger Station, Apache-Sitgreaves National Forests, Alpine, Ariz.

11. *Trail Blazer*, 29 March 1935 and mid-June 1934, Center for Research Libraries, Chicago.

12. *Los Burros Brays*, 28 September 1934, Center for Research Libraries, Chicago.

13. As for the disposition of Hart's buildings, the recollections of Hollis Palmer, a USFS employee on Sitgreaves National Forest (found in history file 1680, Black Mesa Ranger District, Overgaard, Ariz.), suggest that the camp

was moved to Chevalon Canyon to provide start-up buildings for that camp. It makes sense in terms of distance, but the Chevalon camp was not constructed until 1939. It seems unlikely that the buildings were left abandoned at Hart Canyon for up to five years before being moved, when they could have been used for more pressing duty elsewhere on the forest. The buildings could have been taken down and stored until needed at Chevalon, but again it seems unlikely, given the need for shelter for new camps and enrollees all over the forest, that CCC administrators would mothball buildings on the assumption that a future camp would need them. There is no evidence to suggest that the buildings were mothballed. In *Keeping the Boys Busy: Archaeological and Documentary Investigation of* AR-03-12-1391 . . . *a Suggested Historic Context and Research Issues for CCC Erosion Control Sites on the Tonto National Forest* (Tempe, Ariz.: Archaeological Research Services Inc., 1993) Thomas Wright documents that similar CCC buildings elsewhere were simply salvaged and used for other CCC camps—a possible explanation for what happened to Hart Canyon camp too.

14. Flanagan, "My Family and the CCC's in Arizona, 1933–41"; also Marshall Wood, CCC Company 898, interview with the author, 25 October 1999.

15. *Los Burros Brays*, 10 August 1934, Center for Research Libraries, Chicago. Native Americans working on CCC projects were available on the White Mountain Reservation, so it is odd that Los Burros supplied the logs rather than reservation workers.

16. Camp Inspection Reports, F-22-A, 25 July 1936, National Archives Branch Depository, College Park, Md., Records of the CCC, Record Group 35.

17. *Dreamer*, August 1939, Center for Research Libraries, Chicago.

18. Later, the cabin became a tourist attraction with furnishings and memorabilia intact, and a walk-through tour. Sadly, the structure was in the path of the 1990 Dude wildfire and burned to the ground. For an account of Grey's adventures in the Rim Country, see Candace C. Kant, *Zane Grey's Arizona* (Flagstaff: Northland Press, 1984).

19. Camp Inspection Reports, F-23-A, 6 July 1934, National Archives Branch Depository, College Park, Md., Records of the CCC, Record Group 35.

20. "Location and Strength of Civilian Conservation Corps in the 8th Corps Area on August 31, 1933, and Changes among Personnel during the Month," National Archives, files from Archaeological Research Services, Inc., Tempe, Ariz.

21. Francis Cline, interview with the author, 8 March 2001, Young, Ariz. The Cline family has ranched in the Young area since 1920. They also have a connection to the CCC. Francis Cline's grandfather owned the property on which Bar X Ranch camp was constructed. Francis's uncles Ernest and Martin Cline were CCC enrollees who served at Bar X Ranch camp. Ernest contracted pneumonia and died at the camp in July 1933. Francis Cline knows

the location of several of the spring boxes constructed by the CCC northeast of the former camp.

22. Francis Cline, telephone interview with the author, 30 May 2005. Mr. Cline knows the location of many of the remaining toilet house foundations with the CCC imprint in the town of Young.

23. *Eagle's Nest,* 26 October 1935, Center for Research Libraries, Chicago.

24. Kathleen Thomas, transcript summary of interview with Mrs. Floyd (Irene) Andrews, Memo to Clifton Ranger District, Apache-Sitgreaves National Forests, 16 June 1997, Clifton, Ariz.; Kathleen Thomas, interview with the author, 11 December 1999. Ms. Thomas did research on Eagle Creek and other CCC camps for the Alpine Ranger District, Apache-Sitgreaves National Forests.

25. Camp Inspection Reports, F-48-A, 23 October 1937, National Archives Branch Depository, College Park, Md., Records of the CCC, Record Group 35.

26. *Eagle Forester,* 15 August 1936 and 22 August 1936, Center for Research Libraries, Chicago.

27. *Blue Buffalo,* 25 July 1937, Center for Research Libraries, Chicago.

28. Camp Inspection Reports, F-54-A, 14 September 1939 and 1 July 1941, National Archives Branch Depository, College Park, Md., Records of the CCC, Record Group 35. Work projects at Buffalo Crossing were more thoroughly covered in the camp's newspaper, *Blue Buffalo.* See also Alex H. Wagenfehr, interview with unknown person, 30 December 1983, notes on file, no. 2360 (History of CCC), Supervisor's Office, Apache-Sitgreaves National Forests, Springerville, Ariz.

29. Camp Inspection Reports, F-55-A, 7 July 1934, National Archives Branch Depository, College Park, Md., Records of the CCC, Record Group 35.

30. Salmond, *The Civilian Conservation Corps,* 37.

31. Flanagan, "My Family and the CCC's in Arizona," section G.

32. Camp Inspection Reports, F-55-A, 7 July 1934, National Archives Branch Depository, College Park, Md., Records of the CCC, Record Group 35.

33. The *Eagle Forester* of 29 September 1936 reported: "It is expected that Camp F-65-A will be reoccupied this winter, which means we will bring back our Juan Miller Side Camp. It is not known yet which company will occupy F-65-A, but it is expected it will be the same as last year."

34. Camp Inspection Reports, F-75-A, 13 June 1940, National Archives Branch Depository, College Park, Md., Records of the CCC, Record Group 35.

35. "History of Company 863," from files at NACCCA, St. Louis.

36. James E. Cook, "Conservation Corps Answers Call to Duty," *Arizona Republic,* 10 April 1988, E2.

37. "Location and Strength of Civilian Conservation Corps in the 8th Corps Area on June 30, 1937."

38. Flanagan, "My Family and the CCC's in Arizona," section XIV.

39. The company paper, the *Noon Creek Echo*, reported in January 1940 that the company had made many improvements since "the hard working . . . men of Co. 2848 from Springerville moved within its bounds." Such a statement suggests the men had seen duty at Springerville in 1939 before reporting to Noon Creek. It could also mean that the men were from the town of Springerville, but that is unlikely. The town was never big enough to field a company of men. It is known that in 1938 the company began to get replacement workers not from Arizona but from Texas.

40. Flanagan, "My Family and the CCC's in Arizona," section XIV Q.

41. The original road into the area has since been rerouted. The trailhead into the Mount Baldy Wilderness has also been rerouted since the 1930s and the old CCC water pipe system can no longer be found.

42. "Historical Records for CCC Camp Buildings" (East Verde), 30 June 1940, File at Supervisor's Office, Tonto National Forest, Phoenix, Ariz.

43. Camp Inspection Reports, F-77-A, 27 June 1941, National Archives Branch Depository, College Park, Md., Records of the CCC, Record Group 35. Official reports can be written to disguise problems, of course, but enrollees had the right to complain about conditions and to have their complaints added to the official record. While camp inspection records are not complete for most camps, comparisons of records can be useful in identifying common enrollee concerns.

44. Michael Sullivan, archaeologist, Tonto National Forest, interview with the author, Phoenix, Ariz., 11 January 2001.

45. Camp Inspection Reports, F-78-A, 24 June 1941, National Archives Branch Depository, College Park, Md., Records of the CCC, Record Group 35.

46. Ibid.

47. Jim Mendell, interview with the author, Overgaard, Ariz., 5 August 1999; Heather Cooper Provencio, archaeologist, Black Mesa Ranger District, Apache-Sitgreaves National Forests, interview with the author, Overgaard, Ariz., 9 August 1999; Bruce Donaldson, Lakeside District archaeologist, Apache-Sitgreaves National Forests, telephone interview with the author, 13 September 1999. Artifacts at the Wildcat Canyon site found by longtime area resident Jim Mendell and shown to the author suggest a CCC presence, although there is nothing about it in the official record. Evidence found at the site west of Wildcat Canyon is consistent with other camp constructions, but there is no way to prove that this camp was a CCC side camp. If it was, then it took on a more established look, with a flagpole, stone-lined walkways, and a garage-type work area, all of which are still visible on the ground. It is also

unknown if the ridge-top camp was of the tent variety. Temporary sites generally used tents for easy tear-down at the end of a job, and that was probably the case with this site. Since no official record exists of the ridge-top or the canyon site, speculation on its origin, period of use, and manpower will have to wait for more detailed research. As of 2003, archaeological survey work has not been done on either site, and the locations are known to only a few Forest Service officials.

48. Camp Inspection Reports, F-78-A, 24 June 1941, National Archives Branch Depository, College Park, Md., Records of the CCC, Record Group 35.

CHAPTER 3: THE EARLY DAYS AT LOS BURROS: MARSHALL WOOD

1. O. J. Hendricksen, interviewed by Kathleen Thomas, 15 July 1997, transcript on file at Clifton Ranger District, Apache-Sitgreaves National Forests, Clifton, Ariz.

2. Camp Inspection Reports, F-55-A, undated, National Archives Branch Depository, College Park, Md., Records of the CCC, Record Group 35.

3. Camp Inspection Reports, F-48-A, 14 October 1935; F-75-A, 7 July 1941, National Archives Branch Depository, College Park, Md., Records of the CCC, Record Group 35; Lt. Col. Elmer E. Huber (ret.), telephone interview, 21 October 1999. Subsequent references to the interview with the author and undated written communication will appear parenthetically in the text.

4. Otis et al., *The Forest Service and CCC, 1933–42*, 30.

CHAPTER 4: TIME AWAY FROM THE JOB

1. CCC district headquarters received monthly reports from chaplains that noted the camps visited, attendance figures, and other duties performed by the clergy. Copies of such records are extremely hard to find and are not a part of the Record Group 35 files that I have seen in the National Archives. My thanks to Larry Sypolt, West Virginia University, Morgantown, for providing copies from his collection of selected Phoenix District "Monthly Report of Chaplains."

2. Camp Inspection Reports, F-03-A, 25 February 1935; F-55-A, 7 July 1934, National Archives Branch Depository, College Park, Md., Records of the CCC, Record Group 35; see also "Monthly Report of Chaplains," June–October 1936, Sypolt collection, West Virginia University.

3. "Monthly Report of Chaplains" (June 1936), Sypolt collection, West Virginia University; *Chevalon Echo,* 1 November 1939, 18, Center for Research Libraries, Chicago.

4. Camp Inspection Reports, F-23-A, 7 July 1934; F-78-A, 30 June 1941, Na-

tional Archives Branch Depository, College Park, Md., Records of the CCC, Record Group 35.

5. Boyd E. Merrill, "CCC Camp Education Advisor Tells How Boys in Wonderland of Rocks Are Putting in Time at Work and Play," unnamed Arizona newspaper, n.d., 2, Files, Arizona History—1919–1933, Arizona State Capitol Museum Archives, Phoenix.

6. Thim interview.

7. Francis Cline, interview with the author, Young, Ariz., 24 March 2001; Raymond Cline interview; Bud Clark interview. The Cline family's ranching experience in the Young area goes back to the 1920s. The Clines had relatives who served at the camp, and Mr. Clark's father was a sutler at the camp. No camp inspection reports or other government documents exist for the Bar X Ranch CCC camp.

8. *Los Burros Brays,* 5 October 1934, Center for Research Libraries, Chicago; also, Eugene Morris, National Archives specialist, telephone interview with the author, 8 June 2004.

9. Civilian Conservation Corps, "Official Annual . . . 1936," Phoenix District, 8th Corps, Direct Advertising Company, 1936, in Files, Arizona History—1919–1933, Arizona State Capitol Museum Archives, Phoenix, 18.

10. Eugene Gaddy, interview with the author, Blue, Ariz., 10 October 1999.

11. Camp inspection reports from the National Archives for all available camps on the Mogollon Rim and White Mountains indicate that criminal behavior and subsequent disciplinary action by camp commanders was very rare.

CHAPTER 5: PAYSON AND COMPANY 807

1. *Indian Garden's Idyls,* 8 September 1936, 2; 20 October 1936, 6.

2; Camp Inspection Reports, F-23-A, 7 July 1934, National Archives Branch Depository, College Park, Md., Records of the CCC, Record Group 35.

3. Melvin Lorenzen, "A History of Company 807," in Wright, *Keeping the Boys Busy,* E.3.

4. Ibid.

5. Ibid.

6. Ibid.

7. Ibid.

8. The whereabouts of Company 807 in the summer of 1938 is a mystery, according to Thomas Wright in *Keeping the Boys Busy.* Considering the history of the company, it is likely that it was at East Verde, although that is impossible to prove. It is also possible that the company used East Verde as a side camp that summer of 1938.

9. Camp Inspection Reports, F-77-A, 26 June 1941, National Archives

Branch Depository, College Park, Md., Records of the CCC, Record Group 35.

10. "Location and Strength of Civilian Conservation Corps Projects and Work Companies in the 8th Corps Area on May 31, 1941."

11. Camp Inspection Reports, F-77-A, 27 June 1941, National Archives Branch Depository, College Park, Md., Records of the CCC, Record Group 35.

CHAPTER 6: HAPPILY EVER AFTER ON THE BLUE: EUGENE GADDY

1. Eugene Gaddy, interview with the author, Blue, Ariz., 10 October 1999; also Camp Inspection Reports, F-03-A, 16 February 1935, National Archives Branch Depository, College Park, Md., Records of the CCC, Record Group 35.

CHAPTER 7: THE CAMP NEWSPAPER

1. Examples are scattered, but for a typical page, see *Chevalon Echo,* 1 April 1940, 10, Center for Research Libraries, Chicago.

2. *Los Burros Brays,* 31 August 1934, 1; also, *Trail Blazer,* 29 March 1935, Center for Research Libraries, Chicago.

3. *Chevalon Echo,* August 1940, 2, Center for Research Libraries, Chicago.

4. *Chevalon Echo,* 1 February 1940, 5, Center for Research Libraries, Chicago.

5. *Chevalon Echo,* 1 April 1940, 5, Center for Research Libraries, Chicago.

6. Thomas E. Sheridan, *Arizona: A History* (Tucson: University of Arizona Press, 1995), 312.

7. *Indian Garden's Idyls,* n.d., vol. 1, no. 2, Center for Research Libraries, Chicago.

8. Examples abound in camp newspapers as well as in the Camp Inspection Reports. For examples of partnerships with local school districts, see Camp Inspection Reports, F-75-A, "CCC Camp Education Report," 13 June 1940, National Archives Branch Depository, College Park, Md., Records of the CCC, Record Group 35.

CHAPTER 8: A PENNSYLVANIA BOY IN ARIZONA: CHARLES PFLUGH

1. Camp Inspection Reports, F-78-A, 24 June 1941, National Archives Branch Depository, College Park, Md., Records of the CCC, Record Group 35.

2. Ibid.

3. *Chevalon Echo,* 1 December 1939, 7, Center for Research Libraries, Chicago.

4. See also Mary R. Furbee, "Charles Pflugh Calls Year in CCC 'the Best' of His Life," *Times West Virginian,* 1 August 1996, 8A5.

CHAPTER 9: THE FINAL YEARS: RICHARD THIM

1. Thim interview. Some camps had written "behavior" books for new enrollees. For a typical handbook, see Edwin G. Hill, *In the Shadow of the Mountain: The Spirit of the CCC* (Pullman: Washington State University Press, 1990), 169–73; see also CCC camp newspaper the *Hermit,* September 1938, 6, Center for Research Libraries, Chicago.

2. Salmond, *The Civilian Conservation Corps,* 137–38.

3. Richard Thim's wartime service is recognized by Beth Defalco in "They Were D-Day Soldiers," *Arizona Republic,* 6 June 2002, B1.

CHAPTER 10: FAREWELL TO THE CCC

1. Eugene Morris, Textual Archives Services Division, National Archives and Records Administration, College Park, Md., telephone interview, 4 November 1999.

2. Fred Leake and Ray Carter, *Roosevelt's Tree Army: A Brief History of the Civilian Conservation Corps* (St. Louis: NACCCA, n.d.).

3. Camp Liquidation Reports, F-03-A, 4 January 1943; F-78-A, 30 October 1942, National Archives Branch Depository, College Park, Md., Records of the CCC, Record Group 35.

4. Frank Hayes, Clifton District Ranger, Apache-Sitgreaves National Forests, telephone interview with the author, 7 December 1999. Mr. Hayes noticed that the CCC placed inlaid brass plates in the tops of the tables at Juan Miller to show compass direction. On some of those plates the "N" on the north direction sign is backward. It still points north, but the letter is reversed. Perhaps there was poor supervision on the project; or perhaps the young men putting in the signs were in a hurry, or the work was done by enrollees who were not very literate.

5. Fischer, "Love Affair with State Grew Fast," B9.

APPENDIX 2: FIRE LOOKOUTS IN THE RIM COUNTRY

1. Jay M. Price, "It's a Ranger's Life: The Life of a Santa Fe Forest Ranger 1906–1915," USDA Forest Service, Prescott National Forest, Prescott, Ariz., photocopy; see also Baker et al., *Timeless Heritage,* 56.

2. USDA Forest Service, *Cultural Resources Management. Lookouts in the Southwestern Region,* Report 8, September 1989, 32–38.

3. Ibid., 64–125.

Bibliography

INTERVIEWS BY THE AUTHOR

Blumer, Eddie. Young, Arizona, 24 March 2001.

Butler, Kitty Martin. Payson, Arizona, 20 January 2002, 11 June 2004.

Clark, Bud. Young, Arizona, 24 March 2001.

Cline, Francis. Young, Arizona, 24 March 2001, 30 May 2005.

Cline, Raymond. Starr Valley, Arizona, 13 January 2001.

Dallas, Harry, executive director, National Association of CCC Alumni. St. Louis, Missouri, 25 October 2005.

Dean, William (CCC). Camp Hill, Pennsylvania, 30 November 2003.

Donaldson, Bruce, district archaeologist, Lakeside Ranger District, Apache-Sitgreaves National Forests. Telephone interview, 13 September 1999.

Gaddy, Eugene (CCC). Blue, Arizona, 10 October 1999.

Fischer, Elizabeth (Betty) Purdy, wife of Al Purdy (CCC). Telephone interview, 25 February 2002.

Hayes, Frank, Clifton District ranger, Apache-Sitgreaves National Forests. Telephone interview, 7 December 1999.

Huber, Elmer E., Lt. Col. (ret.) (CCC). Sacramento, California, 21 October 1999.

Martin, Linda, chief archaeologist, Apache-Sitgreaves National Forests. Springerville, Arizona, 16 November 1999.

Morris, Gene, Textual Archives Services Division, National Archives and Records Administration. College Park, Maryland, 4 November 1999.

Pflugh, Charles W. (CCC). Fairmont, West Virginia, 30 September 1999, 2 October 1999, 28 October 1999, 16 November 1999, 21 January 2001.

Provencio, Heather Cooper, district archaeologist, Black Mesa Ranger District, Apache-Sitgreaves National Forests. Overgaard, Arizona, 9 August 1999.

Sullivan, Michael, archaeologist, Tonto National Forest. Phoenix, Arizona, 11 January 2001.

Thim, Richard (CCC). Phoenix, Arizona, 30 October 1999.

Thomas, Kathleen. Safford, Arizona, 11 December 1999.

Welch, John, Bureau of Indian Affairs archaeologist, White Mountain Apache Indian Reservation. Telephone interviews, 18 August 1999, 8 June 2004.

Wood, Marshall (CCC). Harper, Texas, 25 October 1999.

GOVERNMENT AGENCIES

Apache-Sitgreaves National Forests:
  Alpine Ranger District
  Black Mesa Ranger District
  Clifton Ranger District
  Lakeside Ranger District
Arizona State Capitol Museum
Coconino National Forest
Coronado National Forest
USDA, Forest Service, Southwestern Regional
  Office, Albuquerque, New Mexico
National Archives and Records Administration
National Park Service
Tonto National Forest

PUBLISHED SOURCES

Baker, Robert D., Robert S. Maxwell, Victor H. Treat, and Henry C. Dethloff. *Timeless Heritage: A History of the Forest Service in the Southwest.* Washington, D.C.: USDA Forest Service, FS-409, 1988.

Booth, Peter M. "Cactizonians: The Civilian Conservation Corps in Pima County, 1933–1942." *Journal of Arizona History* 32 (autumn 1991): 291–332.

———. "The Civilian Conservation Corps in Arizona, 1933–1942." Master's thesis, University of Arizona, 1991.

Burch, Halbert A. "CCC History Underway." *Arizona Historical Society Magazine* 4, no. 6 (1987): 3.

"CCC Educational Programs Discussed at Local Meetings." *Arizona Daily Star,* 24 November 1934. In Files, Arizona History—1919–1933, Arizona State Capitol Museum Archives, Phoenix.

The Civilian Conservation Corps, Coronado National Forest, 1933–1942. USDA Forest Service, Southwestern Region, September 1991.

Collins, William S. *The New Deal in Arizona.* Phoenix: Arizona State Parks Board, 1999.

Cook, James E. "Conservation Corps Answers Call to Duty." *Arizona Republic,* 10 April 1988, E2.

Defalco, Beth. "They Were D-Day Soldiers." *Arizona Republic,* 6 June 2002, B1.

Fischer, Betty Purdy. "Love Affair with State Grew Fast." *Arizona Republic,* 6 January 2002, B9.

Furbee, Mary R. "Charles Pflugh Calls Year in CCC 'the Best' of His Life." *Times West Virginian,* 1 August 1996, 8A5.

HGTV. "America's Homestyles—The Bungalow Special." Broadcast 25 September 1999.

Hill, Edwin G. *In the Shadow of the Mountain: The Spirit of the CCC.* Pullman: Washington State University Press, 1990.

Hoyt, Ray. *"We Can Take It": A Short Story of the C.C.C.* New York: American Book Company, 1935.

Kant, Candace C. *Zane Grey's Arizona.* Flagstaff: Northland Press, 1984.

Leake, Fred E., and Ray S. Carter. *Roosevelt's Tree Army: A Brief History of the Civilian Conservation Corps.* St. Louis, Mo.: NACCCA. Revised March 2000.

Lowe, Sam. "Rustic Respites." *Arizona Republic,* 6 September 1999, D1.

Merrill, Boyd E. "CCC Camp Education Advisor Tells How Boys in Wonderland of Rocks Are Putting in Time at Work and Play." Unnamed, undated Arizona newspaper, 2. In Files, Arizona History—1919–1933, Arizona State Capitol Museum Archives, Phoenix.

National Park Service, Grand Canyon National Park, Arizona. "The Civilian Conservation Corps at the Grand Canyon Village: A Self Guided Walking Tour." Mimeographed.

Official Annual, 1936. Phoenix District, 8th Corps, Civilian Conservation Corps. Direct Advertising Company, 1936.

Otis, Alison T., William D. Honey, Thomas C. Hogg, and Kimberly K. Lakin. *The Forest Service and the Civilian Conservation Corps: 1933–42.* Washington, D.C.: USDA Forest Service, FS-395, 1986.

Purvis, Louis. *The Ace in the Hole: A Brief History of Company 818 of the Civilian Conservation Corps.* Columbus, Ga.: Brentwood Christian Press, 1989.

Salmond, John A. *The Civilian Conservation Corps, 1933–1942: A New Deal Case Study.* Durham: Duke University Press, 1967.

Seymour, Gregory R. *The Civilian Conservation Corps in Southeastern Arizona: An Overview of Fifteen Soil Conservation and Department of Grazing Camps in Graham and Greenlee Counties, Southeast Arizona.* SWCA Archaeological Report No. 95-13. Prepared for Bureau of Land Management, Safford District, Ariz., 13 January 1995.

Sheridan, Thomas E. *Arizona: A History.* Tucson: University of Arizona Press, 1995.

U.S. Department of Agriculture, Forest Service. *Cultural Resources Management. Lookouts in the Southwestern Region.* Report 8, September 1989.

Wright, Thomas E. *Keeping the Boys Busy: Archaeological and Documentary Investigation of AR-03-12-1391, a Civilian Conservation Corps Erosion Control Site in the Tonto Basin, Gila County, Arizona, with a Brief Account of CCC Activities on the Tonto National Forest Lands and a Suggested Historic Context and Research Issues for CCC Erosion Control Sites on the Tonto Na-*

tional Forest. Archaeological Research Services, Project Report No. 93-81, December 1993.

UNPUBLISHED SOURCES

CCC camp newspapers, Center for Research Libraries, Chicago.
Dean, William. Letter to the author, 20 April 2001.
Flanagan, Gene. "My Family and the CCC's in Arizona, 1933–41." NACCCA files, St. Louis, Mo.
Location and Strength of Civilian Conservation Corps in the 8th Corps Area. National Archives, Washington, D.C. Files from Archaeological Research Services, Inc., Tempe, Ariz.
"Monthly Report of Chaplains." CCC Phoenix District, courtesy of Larry Sypolt, Institute for the History of Technology and Industrial Archaeology, West Virginia University, Morgantown.
Palmer, Hollis. Sitgreaves NF History File no. 1680. Black Mesa Ranger District, Overgaard, Ariz.
Pflugh, Charles W. Manuscripts dated 2 October 1999 and 4 November 1999.
Price, Jay M. "It's a Ranger's Life: The Life of a Santa Fe Forest Ranger 1906–1915." USDA Forest Service, Prescott National Forest, Prescott, Ariz.
Read, Kay L. "Life in the Civilian Conservation Corps, Marion Watson." Interview transcript, 21 August 1990. Historical file (Watson), Alpine Ranger Station, Apache-Sitgreaves National Forests, Alpine, Ariz.
Wood, Marshall. Manuscript dated 26 October 1999.

cover art, *100;* and lost enrollee, 99; and move to newer facility, 105; and Charles Pflugh, 82

Civilian Conservation Corps. *See* CCC (Civilian Conservation Corps)

Clark, Elvis, 21

Clay Springs (Ariz.), 20; Charles Pflugh at, 110; Marshall Wood at, 69–70

Clifton (Ariz.), 18–19, and Eagle Creek camp, 43–44; enrollee trips to, 45

Cline, Ernest, 79

Cline, Marvin, 79

Coconino National Forest, 14, 18, 26; Baker Butte fire tower, 132; fire season, 19, 53; Pivot Rock camp, 52, 54

Colcord Road (FR 291), 42, 87

Company 807, 85–90, *89;* at Ashdale–Cave Creek camp, 38; and campground construction, 40; and company flagpole, 40, 126; and company recreation, 73; enrollee demographics, 86; at Indian Gardens camp, 38–40; at Pinal Mountain camp, 38; and road projects, 87, 90. *See also* East Verde camp; Indian Gardens camp

Company 823, 33–34; African Americans in, 34; and company pride, 105; at Fort Huachuca (Ariz.), 33; at Hart Canyon camp, 33–34; Hispanics in, 35; at Los Burros camp, 34–35; Texas enrollees in, 35; and winter camp near Miami (Ariz.), 35; and work for Kinishba Indian pueblo, 36–37

Company 842, 51; and baseball, 80; at Buffalo Crossing camp, 47;

and commemoration of project completion, 103; and fire duty, 47; and road construction, 29; and winter at Blue camp, 30. *See also* Eugene (Gene) Gaddy

Company 847, at F-04-A, 32–33

Company 862: at Juan Miller Camp, 50; at Los Burros camp, 37; at Three Forks camp, 50

Company 863: and enrollment, 53; at Pivot Rock camp, 52

Company 864, *9, 41;* at A-Cross camp, 42; at Bar X Ranch camp, 41–43; and work at Phoenix South Mountain Park, 43

Company 898, at Los Burros camp, 62–64

Company 1830 (veterans unit at Three Forks camp), 48–50

Company 2848: at Greer camp, 55; at Noon Creek camp, 55; and Soil Conservation Service, 55; and WWI veteran in company, 55

Company 2857: and camp newspaper, 97; and company pride, 104; and Eagle Creek camp, 43–46; and Texas recruits, 43

Company 3346, 3; and Arizona arrival, 106; at Chevalon Canyon camp, 58; and Winslow parade, 77

Company 3348: at Nogales (Ariz.), 37; and company pride, 105; and Pennsylvania enrollees, 37; at Williams (Ariz.), 37

Company 3804: at Chevalon Canyon camp, 59; and church services, 75

Control Road (FR 64), Tonto National Forest, 18, 56; and Company 807, 40, 87, 90

Coronado Trail (State Highway 191),

White Mountain Apache Indian Reservation
Fort Bliss (Texas), training at, 62

Rogers, L. W., 13
Roosevelt, Franklin D., 1, 7, 10, 13; and CCC uniforms, 115
Runge, E. C. (Capt.), 67, *67*

Safford (Ariz.), 7, 55, 93, 106
Show Low (Ariz.), rodent control near, 35; and Richard Thim, 118; and Marshall Wood, 69
side camps, 36, 68–70; at Buffalo Crossing, 47; Chamberlain, *89;* at Clay Springs, *69, 70,* 71, 110; at Crescent Lake, 47, *123;* east of Chevalon Canyon camp, 59; East Verde, 40, 56, *57,* 90; at F-04-A, 32; at Gordon Canyon, 39, 87; at Horton Creek, 38–39; Juan Miller, 45, 50; at Mormon Lake, 53; Pivot Rock, 52–53; at Willow Springs, 37
Silver City (N.Mex.): and Eugene (Gene) Gaddy, 91; as staging area, 28
Sitgreaves National Forest, 15, 18; boundary fencing at, 110, 126; Chevalon Canyon and, 106–7; Hart Canyon camp, 33–34; Los Burros camp, 35, 62
Soil Conservation Service (SCS), 7–8. *See also* Company 2848
spike camps. *See* side camps
Springerville (Ariz.), 30, 76, 82, 95; Blue camp open house, 78; and Fred Martin, 23; Richard Thim on, 83–84
State Highway 191. *See* Coronado Trail (State Highway 191)
Strawberry (Ariz.), 18

temporary camps. *See* side camps
Texas enrollees, 6, 101; at Blue camp, 116–17; and Company 807, 86,

90; and Company 862, 37, 50; and Company 863, 52, 54; and Company 864, 41; and Company 1830, 50; and Company 2857, 43–44; at F-04-A, 32–33; Fourth of July, 79; Eugene (Gene) Gaddy and, 91–95; and homesickness, 26, 44, 47, 116; and hometown newspaper, 80; isolation of, 25–26; at Los Burros camp, 35; Marshall Wood and, 62–72; Young (Ariz.) and, 79
Thim, Richard, 3, 16, 78, 114–20, *118, 119,* 122–23; on camp clothing, 115–16; on leave, 117–18; and second tour, 120; on snow sledding, 119; on Springerville, 83–84; on state boundary fence, 116; and winter duty, 17
Three Forks Camp (F-55-A), 37, *49,* 124; camp history, 48–50; church services at, 75; menu at, 65–66; "veterans" company 1830 at, 48–50
Tonto Basin, 42, 87–89
Tonto Creek, 38–39, 73
Tonto National Forest, 18; and Bar X Ranch camp, 40; Company 807 and, 86; and Diamond Point fire lookout, 131, *132;* East Verde camp location, 58; and Young (Ariz.), 79
Tonto National Monument (Ariz.), 73

U.S. Army: and camp construction, 12; and day-to-day camp operation, 1; and opening camps, 27; and site locations, 27; and water for camps, 27–28
U.S. Bureau of Reclamation, 7
U.S. Department of Agriculture, Forest Service. *See* Forest